THE INTRODUCTION TO THE
MAGEE
SYSTEM
OF TECHNICAL
ANALYSIS

THE INTRODUCTION TO THE
MAGEE
SYSTEM
OF TECHNICAL
ANALYSIS

JOHN MAGEE
in a new edition by W.H.C. Bassetti

St. Lucie Press

Boca Raton   London   New York   Washington, D.C.

AMACOM
American Management Association

New York • Atlanta • Boston • Kansas City • San Francisco
Washington, D.C. • Brussels • Mexico City • Tokyo • Toronto

Library of Congress Cataloging-in-Publication Data

Catalog record is available from the Library of Congress

Visit the CRC Press Web site at www.crcpress.com

© 2002 by CRC Press LLC
St. Lucie Press is an imprint of CRC Press LLC

No claim to original U.S. Government works
International Standard Book Number 1-57444-302-X
Printed in the United States of America 1 2 3 4 5 6 7 8 9 0
Printed on acid-free paper

AUTHORS

John Magee (1901–1987), a graduate of MIT and a leading expert on technical analysis, was the founder of the well-known charting and advisory firm of John Magee, Inc. Magee pioneered the concept of analyzing the stock market from an engineering point of view and became known as the Father of Technical Analysis. With Robert Edwards, he coauthored the best selling book, *Technical Analysis of Stock Trends*. Now in its 8th edition, it is considered the definitive work in the field and has more than one million copies in print.

W. H. C. Bassetti, editor and co-author of this book and the 8th edition of *Technical Analysis of Stock Trends*, is an honors graduate of Harvard. His experience spans the modern history of the markets, beginning as a student and client of John Magee in the 1960s through the electronic markets of the present. He was formerly a principal in California's first licensed commodity advisor, CEO of Blair Hull's Options Research, Inc., managing partner of a market maker, and president of an options arbitrage manager. He is presently Adjunct Professor of Finance and Economics at Golden Gate University, where he teaches technical analysis of stock trends.

A SPECIAL
ACKNOWLEDGMENT

Anyone who has engaged in research on issues long dead knows what a nightmare it is to pursue data on the New Haven, or astoundingly(!) IBM before 1968. In fact, if IBM has digital data on its stock prices prior to 1968, I was unable to find it within that corporation (or anywhere else). On the other hand a veritable treasure trove of old data is kept at M.C. Horsey and Company Inc., P.O. Box 2597, Salisbury, MD 21802. On hand-kept ledger cards. M.C. Horsey publishes this data on very long-term monthly charts in "The Stock Picture." I am most indebted to them for use of their IBM data and recommend them to seekers after wisdom and truth who can't find it in real time data.

Special appreciation goes to makers of software packages utilized in preparation of this and previous editions:

AIQ Systems
P.O. Box 7530
Incline Village, NV 89452
702-831-2999
www.AIQ.com

Metastock
Equis International, Inc.
3950 S. 700 East, Suite 100
Salt Lake City, UT 84107
800-882-3040
www.equis.com

TradeStation
Omega Research
14257 SW 119th Avenue
Miami, FL 33186
305-485-7599
www.tradestation.com

ACKNOWLEDGMENTS

First of all, to that irrepressible Maine–iac and distinguished technical analyst Richard McDermott; surfer of the markets, sometime president of John Magee Inc., editor of the first edition of this book and delightful raconteur.

To my invaluable research and editorial assistants, Don Carlos Bassetti y Doyle and Don Pancho Samuelito Bassetti y Doyle who have contributed significantly to this edition. Thanks for the Peaches. Also, the fish.

To my publisher at CRC Press, Drew Gierman and his production staff, especially Pat Roberson, whose professionalism is exemplary, and Michele Berman, who is an excellent, close reader.

To Blair Hull and his staff for generous and helpful support.

To Professor Hank Pruden of Golden Gate University for many favors and kindnesses in the preparation of this and other books.

Members of the Market Technicians Association, especially Shelley, Ed Polokoff, and Jon Knotts at Prophetfinance.com.

And as always, to that modest gentleman, tireless teacher, and master of the craft, John Magee.

FOREWORD

To the uninitiated the field of technical analysis presents an aspect of scientific (or perhaps, pseudo scientific) complexity. If it is not stochastics, it is Bollinger Bands or RSIs or ADXRs or some other jargon-ridden description. Either this is intimidating or it leads the neophyte to expect that if he masters this mélange of tools he will magically, or scientifically, achieve investment success. I regret to inform the reader immediately that there is no Philosopher's Stone.

In reality mathematical or statistical sophistication is not necessary to practice technical analysis in the markets. Any number of little old ladies with a ruler and chart have outperformed any number of Nobel Laureates.

This book is for those just beginning the study of technical analysis, or those conducting a concise review. Its purpose is to initiate the newcomer to technical analysis, to furnish him with sufficient background and knowledge to practice as a beginning and moderately competent technical investor/trader. In addition, it lays out a clear methodology and "system" for trading for the general mid- to long-term investor, and it also lays out a plan of study and self-education for the initiated neophyte who wants a more thorough and detailed mastery of advanced techniques and concepts.

Make no mistake — the intelligent application of technical analysis cannot help but lead to long-term success in investing. But be warned: success involves more than the static use of cookie-cutter principles. It requires, in addition to an intelligent methodology and technique, the ability to see markets clearly and accept immediate realities, and the character and maturity to formulate a plan and then to stick with it when it would appear doomed. Thus, there is not just a rational or consciously intelligent side to investing and trading, there is also, perhaps more important, a psychological, mental side. The best systems in the world are of no use to the investor without the patience to see them through and the discipline to implement them.

WHAT THIS BOOK DOES NOT DO

This book is not a blueprint to riches or infallible investment success. Speaking in general, and speaking specifically, this book does not explain in laborious detail statistical and number-driven systems. Nor does it go into great detail on systems and methods of interest to short-term traders (e.g., day trading methods). Options and futures are introduced but not explored in detail. Background and perspective are offered on all of these subjects and indications are given for more advanced study.

What this book will do is give the newcomer a thorough grasp of chart-oriented technical analysis and the basics of investing following technical methods. And it also offers basic perspective on other important areas of technical analysis (e.g., number-driven techniques) if not advanced detail. With this foundation, readers should be able to manage a general investment portfolio with some confidence and competence. And they should also be able to proceed to further study if they want to continue to develop their capabilities and activities.

THE PLAN OF THE BOOK

This book opens with a concise statement of the principles and basics of technical analysis by the most important master of the craft, John Magee. He expounds on the history of technical analysis, on its most important concepts, such as support/resistance and trends and the patterns that occur over and over in all charts. Then the editor/co-author summarizes and abstracts Magee's work to prepare the reader for the continued study of concepts and tools developed in large part after Magee practiced. Included is material on Magee's methods for managing portfolios and controlling risk, including a description of his stop systems. To my knowledge there are no better stop systems extant.

Then this book presents a brief survey of number-driven technical methods, along with descriptions of Candlestick charting and Point and Figure charting. Magee follows with a semantical discussion of his method, calculated to give readers a rational confidence in the process.

PURPOSE OF THE BOOK

My intention is that the conscientious reader should emerge from the book with a well-rounded grasp of Magee-type analysis and be able profitably to manage a mid- to long-term investment portfolio — without, of course, attempting anything fancy or clever.

Not to discriminate against the fancy and clever (that being my history), racy traders will find here the indispensable perspective and foundation on which to rest further studies. And the direction these studies should take will be pointed out to them. Traders need to know the same thing investors need to know. They also must know other things which the investor will profit from knowing. Some of this is presented here.

To this end, this book includes appendices on Directed Further Study as well as on Resources for all types of investors. Included also is material on suggested trading plans for all different types of investors — plungers to the somnolent.

EDITORIAL METHODS AND ORGANIZATION OF THE BOOK

The basic material of this book was written by John Magee, some was written by the redoubtable and distinguished technician Richard McDermott, and the modernized parts were written by myself as Magee's diligent student. I consider my thought and methods to be essentially extensions of what I learned from Magee, supplemented by experience with many developments in statistics, markets, and technology. I have called these various ideas about risk, portfolio, and trading systems Pragmatic Portfolio Theory, as it seems to me that Magee was the essence of pragmatic. These ideas are introduced and briefly covered here and should be sufficient for the average general investor. The theory is more fully discussed in the 8th edition of Edwards and Magee's classic work on the subject, *Technical Analysis of Stock Trends*.

In view of the fact that this volume is a relaxed and informal presentation of ideas more fully expressed in Edwards and Magee's classic, I have not been overly rigorous academically in the changes and additions I have made to this book. Readers will, in general, readily distinguish my work from Magee's. I have used italics where I have directly intruded on his text. I have also made moderate changes in the organization of Magee's text to fit a pedagogical plan I have found effective in teaching technical analysis seminars at Golden Gate University and the University of California, Berkeley, Extension.

ABOUT GENDER

Female readers will note that the usage of "her system," "she will," and so on does not appear in this book and perhaps think Magee and me chauvinist pigs. Quite the contrary. I quote here from my foreword to the 2nd edition of Magee's *General Semantics of Wall Street* (charmingly renamed according to the current fashions, *Winning the Mental Game on Wall Street*):

"About Gender in Grammar

"Ich bin ein feminist. How could any modern man, son of a beloved woman, husband of an adored woman and father of a joyful and delightful daughter not be? I am also a traditionalist and purist in matters of usage, grammar and style. So where does that leave me and my cogenerationalists, enlightened literary (sigh) men (and women) with regards to the use of the masculine pronoun when used in the general sense to apply to the neuter situation?

"In *Dictionary of Modern American Usage,* Garner notes: 'English has a number of common-sex general words, such as *person, anyone, everyone,* and *no one,* but it has no common-sex singular personal pronouns. Instead we have *he, she,* and *it.* The traditional approach has been to use the masculine pronouns *he* and *him* to cover all persons, male and female alike. ...The inadequacy of the English language in this respect becomes apparent in many sentences in which the generic masculine pronoun sits uneasily.'

"Inadequate or not it is preferable to s/he/it and other bastardizations of the English language. (Is it not interesting that 'bastard' in common usage is never used of a woman, even when she is illegitimate?) As for the legitimacy of the usage of the masculine (actually neuter) pronoun in the generic, I prefer to lean on Fowler, who says, 'There are three makeshifts: first *as anybody can see for himself or herself;* second, *as anybody can see for themselves;* and third, *as anybody can see for himself.* No one who can help it chooses the first; it is correct, and is sometimes necessary, but it is so clumsy as to be ridiculous except when explicitness is urgent, and it usually sounds like a bit of pedantic humor. The second is the popular solution; it sets the literary man's (!) teeth on edge, and he exerts himself to give the same meaning in some entirely different way if he is not prepared to risk the third, which is here recommended. It involves the convention (statutory in the interpretation of documents) that where the matter of sex is not conspicuous or important the masculine form shall be allowed to represent a person instead of a man, or say a man (*homo*) instead of a man (*vir*).'

"Politically correct fanatics may rail, but so are my teeth set on edge; thus I have generally preserved the authors' usage of the masculine for the generic case. This grammatical scourge will pass and be forgotten and weak willed myn (by which I intend to indicate men and women) who pander to grammatical terrorists will in the future be seen to be stuck with malformed style and sentences no womyn will buy. What would Jane Austen have done, after all?

"About Gender in Investors

"And, as long as we are on the subject of gender, we might as well discuss, unscientifically, gender in investors. Within my wide experience as a trading advisor, teacher, and counselor it strikes me that the women investors I have known have possessed certain innate advantages over the men. I know there are women gamblers. I have seen some. But I have never seen in the markets a woman plunger (shooter, pyramider, pie eyed gambler). And I have known many men who fit this description (and in fact have done some of it myself). I have also noted among my students and clients that as a group women seem to have more patience than men as a group. I refer specifically to the patience that a wise investor must have to allow the markets to do what they are going to do."

I have found the previous edition of this marvelously concise little book an ideal beginning textbook, a perfect first step to further study in the bigger more complete, more complex *Technical Analysis of Stock Trends*. The rearrangements I have made of the material fall naturally into the teaching plan I use in seminars.

W.H.C. Bassetti
San Francisco

CONTENTS

SECTION III: MAGEE'S METHODOLOGY: RISK MANAGEMENT, PORTFOLIO MANAGEMENT, AND RHYTHMIC TRADING. PRAGMATIC PORTFOLIO THEORY FROM BASSETTI

The Magee method is briefly summarized, and Bassetti develops and articulates Magee's ideas of rhythmic investing, portfolio management, and risk management and control.

SECTION IV: OTHER TECHNICAL ANALYSIS TOOLS: NUMBER-DRIVEN TECHNIQUES, CANDLESTICKS, AND POINT-AND-FIGURE-CHARTING — ALGORITHMIC TRADING

Charting is the original form of technical analysis, the basic discipline. With the development of the computer, other forms of technical analysis have evolved — number-driven (or statistical) analysis, candlesticks, and point-and-figure analysis.

SECTION V: CONSIDERATIONS FOR TRADERS/ INVESTORS OF WHATEVER STRIPE — DAY TRADERS TO LONG-TERM INVESTORS

Implications of technical analysis are put in context for various kinds of traders/investors, from short-term traders to long-term investors: What kind of analysis is appropriate for whom. Sample trading plans for these various categories of traders are discussed.

SECTION VI: TRADING IS ONLY HALF SYSTEMS AND METHODS — THE OTHER 90% IS MENTAL

Magee explores the philosophical and psychological aspects of stock market trading and investing.

SECTION VII: APPENDICES

Market wisdom. After basic training and drill the army enters the battle. How well does the theory and method hold up in the heat of combat? Also, the necessities of manual Tekniplat charting. Indications for further study and resources for traders/investors.

I

A BRIEF HISTORY OF DOW THEORY AND THE FOUNDATIONS OF TECHNICAL ANALYSIS

Magee summarizes the basics of technical analysis, its origins in Dow Theory, something of its philosophy, and a brief discussion of its primary tool, the bar chart.

Dow Theory, deriving from original editorials in the *Wall Street Journal* by Charles Dow, stated that the near future of the economy — and of the stock market in general, could be forecast by observing the average behavior of 30 industrial stocks and 20 transportation stocks. When these averages advanced in concert a Bull Market was in effect and, conversely, when they declined in concert a Bear Market was in effect. Signals cast off by these two averages may be used as buy-and-sell indicators and have been for 100 years. Buying and selling on Dow signals would have netted $362,212.98 in 103 years on an initial $100 investment as opposed to $39,685.03 realized from a buy-and-hold plan.

Dow Theory is wholly a technical method. Technical analysts saw that principles of Dow Theory could be applied to individual stocks and, using bar charts, developed the theory and have applied it productively for more than half a century. The definitive statement of chart-based technical analysis is Edwards & Magee's *Technical Analysis of Stock Trends* (1st ed., 1948; 8th ed., 2001). Contrary to the beliefs of academic random walkers, trends occur in the markets and the most productive investment methodology identifies and profits from these trends, using bar charting as its basic tool.

1

BASIC TENETS OF TECHNICAL ANALYSIS AS EVOLVED FROM DOW-JONES THEORY AND THE BAR CHART, TOOL OF TECHNICAL ANALYSIS

John Magee's Inc.'s objective has always been to forecast individual stock prices — not the "overall" stock market. Investors buy individual stocks, not the "market" — their profits (or losses) reflect how well those stocks do. (*Magee, of course, wrote this statement and practiced before it was possible for the general investor to "buy the market" by purchasing ishares or DJIA futures, instruments which effectively allow the investor to "buy the market." These instruments are explored later. The purposes and methods Magee discusses remain valid not only for individual stocks but also for the averages themselves.*) Although it is often the case that the vast majority of stocks move in the same direction as the market, it is not always so. Certain groups may lead a market move whereas others may lag or not participate at all. And, even within a group of stocks such as airlines or steel, for example, certain stocks may move ahead of, with, or actually lag behind their own group.

The basic tenets of technical analysis were first put forth by Charles Dow, editor of the *Wall Street Journal* and creator of the Dow-Jones averages. By analyzing the behavior of the industrial and rail averages, Dow developed a theory — the famous Dow Theory — by which he sought to forecast the major direction of the stock market from the price behavior of these indices.

THEORIES AND ASSUMPTIONS

The foundations for modern technical analysis of stock trends were laid by Charles Henry Dow, a founder and the first editor of the *Wall Street Journal*. During his tenure as editor, from July 8, 1889, until his death on December 4, 1902, Dow published his observations on the market and its likely future direction based on the interactions between the industrial and railroad averages. These editorials constitute the solid core of present-day Dow Theory. The industrials represent the strongest and biggest companies, called "blue chips" or primary issues. These companies are in goods and services. The transports are secondary issues that move goods and people such as rails, trucks, barges, and airlines. The two basic assumptions of Dow Theory technical analysis are as follows:

1. The averages, in their day-to-day fluctuations, discount everything known, everything foreseeable, and every condition that can affect the supply of or the demand for corporate securities; and
2. The market moves in trends, upward or downward, over time.

The fundamental premise of technical analysis is that it is possible to identify and predict the continuations and turning points in market trends, to evaluate relative strength or weakness in the market, and to profit from the application of that analysis.

The central method of Dow Theory involves examining the co-movements of two averages, such as the Dow-Jones industrials and the Dow-Jones transportations, for "confirmations." One average is usually regarded as the primary one and the other as the confirming index. Confirmation occurs when, for instance, the industrials reach a high above their previous high, and the transportations do likewise around the same time. The trend in the averages is held far more likely to continue when confirmation is present than when it is absent.

In addition, technicians have used the Dow-Jones transportation average as a confirming indicator to the industrials since the days of Charles H. Dow. (Confirmation — in other words if one average is going up, or down, the other should be going in the same direction to confirm.) At that time, the junior average consisted only of railroad stocks. The industrials were considered an index of productive activity and the rails one of distributive activity. Both of these should be sound in order to have a healthy economy and, hence, a healthy stock market. Although the rails do not "move the nation" now as they did then, today's transportation index still provides a supplementary barometer of speculation in the market and, therefore, continues to be useful.

Chart 1. Dow-Jones Averages Chart Showing Divergences and Confirmations of Industries by Transportation. In May and June the industrials and the transportations part ways, that is diverge — an ominous sign for the Dow, and also for the entire market. The industrials continue merrily along waiting until the fateful month of October to confirm the transportation move. Both averages react and the Dow goes to its all-time high with the transportations once again diverging in November and the joint downtrend reaching mutual confirmation in March 2000. The consequences and reflections of this action in the averages may be seen in Chart 4.

The technician's assumption is that if confirmation occurs between the industrials and either of these supplementary indicators (or more strongly, both), a trend under way would be likely to continue. If confirmation were not present, the averages would be said to be "out of gear" (or divergent), and the trend in the industrials would be less likely to continue. The usefulness of this, if it were true, would not be confined to the narrow Dow-Jones averages alone. Correlation among all the major averages is of a high degree and well established historically. The technician's assumption about confirmations and trends appeared to us to be easy enough to test. Confirmations are visible on charts, as are subsequent movements in the averages. Robert D. Edwards and I, therefore, set out to test (in *Technical Analysis of Stock Trends*) whether any statistically valid, identifiable connection exists between confirmations and subsequent continuations of trends.

Several of the basic principles of technical analysis extended from Dow Theory of overall stock market behavior and applied to individual stocks, *however, deserve attention. These principles are, in brief, the foundations of technical analysis, as explained below. Dow Theory, although not completely objective (i.e., reducible to an uncontested algorithm), shows considerable power in practice. An investor following the long-term trading signals of the Dow, from its inception in 1897 up to 2000, would have realized $362,212.98 on an initial investment of $100, whereas an investor who bought $100 of the average at its inception and held it to its high in 1999 would have realized $39,685.03.*

BASIC TENETS OF TECHNICAL ANALYSIS

The first major principle of technical analysis is that the market action of an individual stock reflects all the known factors affecting that stock's future. Among the factors, and expressed in its chart, are the general market conditions which influence all stocks to a greater or lesser degree, as well as the particular conditions applying to the particular stock, including the trading of insiders. A basic tenet of the Dow Theory is that the averages discount everything (except "Acts of God" — *and Alan Greenspan*). In technical analysis, price and volume are the great "data reducers of the stock market" — for individual stocks as well as for the averages. By concentrating on the interpretation of price and volume patterns only, and by disregarding the never-ending stream of corporate information, advisors' opinions, rumors, and tips and hunches from well-meaning friends, the technical analyst approaches common stock selection in a systematic manner, ideally suited for fast-moving markets in which timely judgment and decisive action invariably spell the difference between success and failure.

The second basic principle or premise is that stocks move in trends.

The third basic principle is that volume goes with the trend. In an uptrend, volume rises as prices rise and declines as prices decline. Contrary behavior by a stock in an uptrend may signal an important topping out, or reversal, in the near future. For those who think this is obvious, we would point out that it is frequently not the case. Price peaks and valleys often occur during periods of low trading activity. This provides the technician with a clear signal that buying or selling pressure is abating and a new price trend is forming.

The fourth, and last, basic premise of technical analysis is that a trend, once established, tends to continue. Until such time as its reversal has been signaled, a trend is assumed to continue in effect. This proposition is essentially stating an important probability — the likelihood that the next move in a stock will be in the same direction as the previous one.

STOCK IN UPTREND

An uptrend is considered to be in force as long as each successive rally reaches a higher price than the one before it, and each successive reaction stops at a higher level than the previous reaction. A similar (*reversed or mirror image*) definition holds for a downtrend.

We divide a trend into three subcategories:

1. The major trend usually lasts a year or more and results in appreciation or depreciation of 20% or more.
2. The intermediate trend operates in the opposite direction of the major trend, usually retracing one half or less of the prior movement in the direction of the major trend. It is often referred to as an intermediate reaction.
3. Minor trends consist of day-to-day fluctuations which are unimportant except as they combine to form larger trends.

For our purposes, it is more instructive to discuss some of the basic assumptions a technician makes in interpreting a chart. This discussion must begin with the relationship of volume and stock price. The rule of thumb is that when stock price and volume rise together, there is sufficient buying pressure to indicate an uptrend. Conversely, although not as directly proportional, price declines will be accompanied by increasing volume if there is sufficient selling pressure to indicate a downtrend. *It is, however, not necessary that volume increase on declines to definitively indicate a downtrend. Price alone can indicate this.*

Here are three charts of stocks (charts 2, 3, and 4) in normal trends, such as those seen every day in the markets. One is an uptrend, one a downtrend, and one a sideways trend.

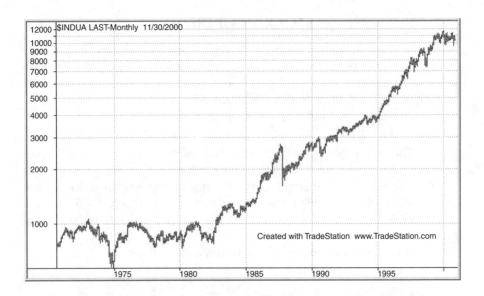

Chart 2.   The Dow Industrials Uptrend. Here is the greatest uptrend in the history of the U.S. markets — the Great Clinton–Gore bull market. A complex of factors combined to produce the most important market in U.S. history. The benefits of computer technology, the rush to the Internet, the incredible prosperity of the people as a whole, and not least the fiscal responsibility of the Clinton–Gore administration, which for the first time since the 1950s balanced the budget and began to pay down the enervating debt produced in the Reagan years. Technicians generally turn a deaf ear to analyses of this kind. And usually for the immediate moment and for the short-term purposes of investing and trading they should. But secular factors of this kind are worth noting, if not trading on. Trading and investing takes place for most investors in a much more limited time frame.

Chart 3. Xerox, in a Downtrend. Bull trends require labor and time and blood sweat and tears. Bear trends are effortless and fall to earth, in many cases, like a punctured hot-air balloon. Often it was hot air which created the bull trend. *But virtually always an important trend line is broken before the bear trend begins. This is a common downtrend* — after all a downtrend must begin from up. And almost always will be ragged rather than regular, especially in modern markets where investors are so quick to flee the least sign of weakness.

Chart 4. Dow-Jones Industrials in a Sideways Trend, with a moving average line. At the turn of the millennium as the great bull market topped, the Dow produced a constellation of formations which all added up to the same thing — sideways trend. A long-term moving average vividly illustrates the nature of a sideways trend — the price see-saws back and forth across it effectively destroying any trend following system which does not know to quit trading in sideways trends. In these situations traders can make money shorting the top of the trading range, covering and buying the bottom — as long as they know when to quit this tactic, because eventually the price will fall out or break out and bite a trader who overuses this tactic.

HOW TECHNICIANS USE BAR CHARTS TO STUDY THE MARKETS

The purpose of this discussion is to explain the nature of the bar chart, something of the history and development of the use of charts in the evaluation of securities, and the philosophy and rationale of charting. In later chapters we discuss some of the technical patterns seen on charts and their use and interpretation, methods and details of application and use, and comments and suggestions as to the setting up and maintaining of daily charts.

What Is A Bar Chart?

A bar chart is one of the many methods of representing information in graphic form. It consists of a rectilinear grid on which two variables can be plotted. Thus, the vertical axis might be scaled to represent "miles per hour" of a moving automobile and the horizontal axis, the "rate of gasoline consumption." The vertical axis might be "total number of employees" in various industries and the horizontal axis "average wage of employees." In many kinds of engineering, sociological, and economic problems, the horizontal axis represents time (hours, days, months, etc.), and the vertical axis measures the magnitude of a second variable such as population, net income, pressure, or whatever data are under examination. In the study of securities, bar charts are widely used to show the record of price trends and fluctuations over time. These charts can be adapted to any type of financial market: stocks, bonds, warrants, debentures, commodities, etc. They can be used for long periods, perhaps covering many years, or they may be focused down to short-term trends on a daily or even hourly basis. (*With today's technology, charts may be computer-generated on every tick of the market in real time.*)

In charting security prices, the high and low prices for the day (if it is a daily chart that is being run) are plotted on the line that represents the particular day, and the high and low are connected by a vertical line. Usually, the closing or last price for the day is shown as a cross-line on this vertical range. It is also possible to show both the opening price and the closing price, using a short line to the left of the vertical range for the opening, and a short line to the right to indicate the close. The volume of trading may be shown on a separate scale near the bottom of the sheet, directly under the vertical lines showing the daily price range. For weekly charts or monthly charts, the procedure is exactly the same except that each horizontal interval represents a week or a month instead of a day.

Because the horizontal scale on the chart provides a "calendar," it is possible to enter any other data directly on the chart. This includes, of course, dividend or ex-distribution dates, the dates of stock splits, any data that might seem important as to earnings, mergers, and announcements of new products, and so on. By noting on the proper date the purchase or sale of a stock and the price paid or received, a record of these transactions will be right on the chart — which will make it easy to check the status of a transaction and the profit or loss on it. Moreover, this record will serve as a valuable study later as to the degree of success of decisions.

The Uses and Applications of Charts

Before anyone can use any method in business, finance, science, or any other field, and before he can judge properly the usefulness of the method, he should have some background of theory and the goals he hopes to reach. At this point we want to consider some of this important background.

We have already spoken of the use of charts simply as a record of stock prices and trading volume — in other words, the market action of the stock — and also of the convenience of recording other data on the chart itself rather than in separate notebooks or tables. A more important use of the chart is in backchecking the results of one's judgment, building up a body of firsthand experience in a form that can be consulted and analyzed later, and in acquiring better perception — learning from both one's past successes and failures.

To many people, the stock market is a confusing and confused melee in which prices move helter-skelter without rhyme or reason. But this confusion is, to some extent, a confusion in their own minds, because they do not understand the complicated forces and the detail of procedure that actually cause stock prices to advance or decline. They might feel the same sense of meaningless movement that a visitor to a textile mill might feel the first time he saw the operation of an automatic loom. He might not understand at first sight that the strange shifts of the jacquard mechanism were not meaningless but were directed toward the orderly creation of a definite pattern in the cloth which would have meaning to anyone when he saw the finished product.

Groups of students in technical analysis of stock trends are often skeptical as to the meaning or orderliness of the market at the first or second lectures in a course. When they discover, as they do, that the long-term trends of stocks, covering a period of a number of years, show definite trends which often appear as straight-line channels on semilogarithmic charting paper, they are likely to be overcome with enthusiasm. Sometimes it is necessary to warn them that the existence of trends, though true, is not the entire key to success in the stock market but merely one of a number of important facts that appear in the study of charts. In this field, "a little" knowledge can be a dangerous thing indeed.

The question, at this point, is, of course, whether the charts have predictive value — whether they can be of help in planning the purchase or sale of stocks with respect to the future movement of stock prices. As to this we have a definite opinion that they do. But anyone planning to use charts in his own financial planning should understand as thoroughly as possible their theory and application. He should learn some of the characteristic behaviors of charted stocks, check and verify what he has read and heard by his own current observations, and have some idea of what may be abstracted or surmised from a chart, and with what degree of dependability.

THE BLOODLESS VERDICT OF THE MARKETPLACE

Following the line of reasoning in the preceding sections, especially that part that touches on the difficulty of knowing all about a corporation or about the market as a whole, we realize that the most dependable criterion of value in the practical sense of what one must pay, or what one can get for something (whether it should be shares of stock, bushels of wheat, land, houses, automobiles, or whatever), is the free speculative auction in which the bids and offers of prospective buyers and sellers determine the price. Whether the reasons behind these bids and offers are sound, reasonable, or wise has nothing to do with the fact that the price is determined by them, and any investor is at liberty to take it or leave it.

There is an implication here that men who are putting their own hard-earned cash on the line to support their opinions are likely to have serious reasons for doing so; there is at least a presumption that the composite of these opinions, the consensus as represented by the price at a given moment, may be the most realistic expression of value we can hope to get.

Therefore, following this line of reasoning, we must assume that the current price of the stock represents all that is known, or believed, or hoped, or feared, in connection with the present value or future probable value of that stock.

THE CHARTS SIMPLY REFLECT HUMAN EVALUATION

The question is sometimes raised as to whether a stock chart will reflect unreasoning emotional states of mind on the part of investors. That is surely true at times. There have been "crazy" booms in stocks, and there have been equally "crazy" collapses and panics. But, the fact that these market actions cannot always be supported by factual reports and statistics does not make them any less important. When the price of a stock starts to climb or when the bottom falls out of it, it is best to take appropriate action, recognizing that an important move is taking place, rather than trying to hold back the tide because it does not seem to make any sense. In a surprising number of cases, the move eventually does prove to make sense; the collective judgment of the market is extremely sensitive and perceptive as to probable changes in production, earnings, dividends, and other matters affecting the affairs of a company.

If a market move turns out to be premature or false, if the expected, or hoped for, or feared, developments do not come about, it is still true that one cannot argue with the tape. It is best, we feel, to accept the facts regardless of the reasons, assuming that in most cases the reasoning behind the move is sound.

One other question remains which we feel has always been given more weight than it deserves, especially by those who have not studied too long or too deeply. The question is whether the movement may represent merely the manipulative operations of dishonest traders, or whether, through false rumors or merely through the fact that something seems to be happening, the movement snowballs and accelerates on its own momentum.

As far as dishonest manipulation is concerned, this has never been an entirely safe or easy thing, even in the "bad old days" when no punches were barred. Today, with the various regulatory laws and the rules of procedure in the important Exchanges, plus the self-protective, self-regulation of the reputable brokerage houses, it is more difficult. Still, as the various insider trading trials prove, there will always be a dishonest element in the market.

Nor do we believe that the important market moves are merely the result of rumor, collective hysteria, and emotional confusion. There are too many hardheaded men, both individuals and traders for institutions, who are prepared to check and counterbalance an entirely capricious or irrational move. We would question whether the recommendations of brokers or investment advisory services, or the statements of newspaper writers or radio and TV analysts, or the self-reflexive action of technical factors are major elements in important market moves. In all this, in all the changes shown in the charts (which are a picture of what is actually happening in the market and which are indirectly a portrayal of what the collective investing public is perceiving), we are dealing with speculation. In this connection, we are using the word in the particular sense in which *Webster's Ninth New International Dictionary* defines it, in the first definition of the word as in current use: "The faculty, act, or process of intellectual examination or investigation." This is the proper and legitimate function of a market and in no way implies any dishonorable or unfair practice. The word, as Webster here defines it, is merely synonymous with evaluation, and it is in this sense that we use it in this treatise.

THE TECHNICAL PICTURE

We have spoken of the chart as a "picture," a picture of the composite evaluations going on in the minds of many people. We have spoken of the chart as "a tool." In spite of the possible effect of buying or selling by some technicians who use charts, we do not believe that "the chart makes the market go." On the contrary, we believe that the market makes its own complex evaluation, and the chart reflects this continually changing appraisal.

In general, as Charles H. Dow discovered before the turn of the century, the market tends to anticipate expected conditions. Therefore (with Dow), we assume that when the market or some particular stock is moving strongly into higher ground, it is because people are anxious to buy it and are willing to bid more for it. Conversely, when a stock is slumping to new lows, it suggests that people are pessimistic about its future and are prepared to take less for it in order to get it off their hands.

This, as we will see, appears to run somewhat counter to the ordinary idea of buying something while it is cheap and selling it when it is dear. We read so often of stocks that are overpriced. Yet the man who sells these overpriced stocks, or sells them short, often finds that the upward trend continues for months or years. Similarly, the investor who attempts to buy at the bottom is often disappointed, because the stock which has been in trouble for some time is quite likely to continue to slump.

Something else about the low-priced stocks should be mentioned here. It seems reasonable to suppose that stock that once sold at $100 a share, which has dropped to $10 a share, must be at or near its ultimate bottom. An investor will sometimes argue that because it has already dropped 90 points from 100 to 10, it cannot drop more than 10 points at the most. But this is a trap, and a dangerous one. Consider that you have $10,000 to invest. This would have bought you 100 shares of the stock at the price of $100. When the stock dropped to 10, your accrued loss would have been 90%, or $9,000. But if you should wait, and then buy the stock at $10, and it should drop 9 points to $1, your loss would have once again been 90%, and if you had used the same capital of $10,000 to buy 1,000 shares at $10, you would have suffered a loss of $9,000, the same as in the first case. On a percentage basis (which is what the logarithmic scales show clearly) there is no bottom to the chart, and no top — no limit to what portion of your capital you could make or lose. (*For an interesting practical lesson on this final point see Appendix A, Some Selected John Magee Letters, page 144.*)

II

THE CENTRAL
CONCEPTS AND
VOCABULARY OF
TECHNICAL ANALYSIS

Magee concisely recounts the central concepts of technical analysis, support and resistance, trends, and some of the important patterns that occur in normal market activity. Patterns of both long-term and short-term importance are displayed. In addition to an explanation of this basic "vocabulary," the Magee system of stops is briefly explained by Bassetti.

In any free-market auction marketplace, the item being traded seeks a consensus price. If more people want to sell than want to buy it, it will decline in price. And vice versa. The battle between buyers and sellers will leave bodies on the field — the buyer who bought at 100 and saw a price decline of 20 points and, smarting, seized the opportunity to get out when the stock got back close to 100. Thus does resistance form. And support forms when a majority of the traders believe that the stock is underpriced at 90. The interplay between these levels of support and resistance takes identifiable patterns (rectangles, triangles, flags, etc.) depending on the strength of convictions of the two sides. As one side or the other gains additional adherents, resistance, for example, will be overcome, and a trend, or the continued movement of prices in one direction, will result.

In addition to patterns that form over weeks or months, markets continually display short-term patterns of interest — gaps, spikes, reversal days. These can have immediate importance as well as importance for the longer term.

It is all very well to see one's stocks go up. When do you sell? The explanation of stops which is given in this section reveals the best thinking of one of the most respected advisors in the history of U.S. markets.

In view of the fact that frequent reference will be made to certain terms definitions will be offered here. *Basing points*, which are explored in depth in Chart 27, are reaction points in a trend used for drawing trend lines and calculating progressive stops. The *MEI*, or *Magee Evaluative Index*, is an index calculated by analyzing a sector or Average by deconstructing it into strong neutral and weak percentages. *Ishares* are stock-like instruments which represent a small percentage of a major index, for example, the *DIA* is 10% of the Dow Jones Industrials.

2

IMPORTANT PRACTICAL CONCEPTS: SUPPORT AND RESISTANCE

For the purposes of this discussion, we may define support as buying — actual or potential — sufficient in volume to halt a downtrend in prices for an appreciable period. In other words, it is where the buying is. Resistance is the antithesis of support. It is selling, actual or potential, sufficient in volume to satisfy all bids and, hence, stop prices from going higher for a time. Support and resistance, as they are defined, are nearly, but not quite, synonymous with supply and demand, respectively.

A support level, or zone or band, is a price level at which sufficient demand for a stock appears to halt a downtrend temporarily at least, and possibly reverse it (i.e., start prices moving up again). A resistance level, or zone or band, by the same token, is a price level at which sufficient supply of a stock is forthcoming to stop, and possibly turn back, its uptrend. There is, theoretically and nearly always actually, a certain amount of supply and a certain amount of demand at any given price level. (The relative amount of each varies according to circumstances and determines the trend.) But a support range represents a concentration of demand, and a resistance range represents a concentration of supply.

According to the foregoing definitions, the top boundary of a horizontal congestion pattern, such as a rectangle, is a resistance level, and its bottom edge a support level (*see Chart 5*); the top line of an ascending triangle is unmistakably a resistance level.

Pullbacks and throwbacks — the quick return moves we noted as developing so often shortly after a breakout from head-and-shoulders formations or other area patterns — exemplify the principles of support

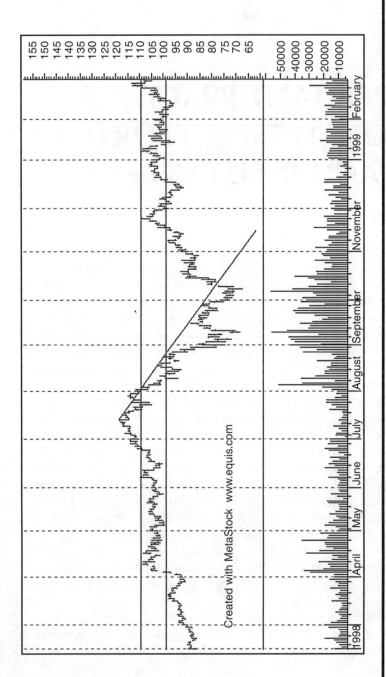

Created with MetaStock www.equis.com

Chart 5. American Express, Support and Resistance Illustration. This chart of American Express vividly illustrates the phenomenon of support and resistance, as marked by the horizontal lines. For months price bounces off the resistance at 110 and when repulsed finds support around 99. An almost perfect bull trap is executed in July — almost perfect because the shrinkage in volume on the breakout and top is a sharp warning sign of something amiss. Rising volume as price falls from the top is another warning sign. Then the huge increase in volume in early August is the third strike. The exaggerated volume from August to October as disappointed bulls liquidate their holdings allows the breakout in mid October, and then the stock goes happily back to its support/resistance range.

and resistance. When prices break down, for example, out of a descending triangle, the horizontal lower boundary of the formation, which was originally a demand line, promptly reverses its role and becomes a resistance line. Any attempt to put prices back up through it after a decisive breakout is stopped by supply at or near the line. By the same token, the neckline of a head-and-shoulders top, which was a demand line, becomes a resistance level after it has been broken. The top, or supply line of the rectangle, becomes a support line after prices have pushed above it on volume and by a decisive margin.

Major corrections or crashes, such as the ones in 1929, 1962, (*1987, 1998, and 2001*) can change supply and demand zones fast. Panics, once they get under way, seem to sweep away all potential support in their calamitous plunges until they exhaust themselves in a general market-selling climax.

Another basic premise of technical analysis is that each stock has a level of primary price support and resistance — in short, a price range indicating an historical balance of buying and selling pressure. In stocks with a record of volatile price activity, the range will be broader than that of a stock whose price has not fluctuated dramatically. The primary support and resistance levels are most obvious in stocks that have remained inactive for lengthy periods. Technicians call this channeling. If a stock price violates primary support or penetrates previous resistance, particularly on an increase in trading volume, the technician assumes that a trend is forming. In the case of inactive or channeling stocks, such a breakout often indicates dramatic future price activity.

Technical analysis also reveals the existence of secondary price support levels. Stock prices do not move in a straight line. Within an uptrend, they advance, retreat, and then advance again. Conversely, during a downtrend, the pattern is decline, partial rebound, and further decline. Secondary price support levels are the price ranges to which stock prices either rise or fall before resuming the dominant trend. They are not static but, rather, move with the stock price. In the case of an uptrend, when a stock price falls below the previous secondary support level, the technician is alerted to a potential change and, perhaps, reversal of the dominant trend.

Overpage we illustrate the mechanics of support and resistance formation.

DIAGRAMS ILLUSTRATING MECHANICS OF SUPPORT AND RESISTANCE

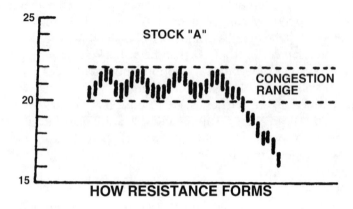

Diagram 1.   How Resistance Forms. Here we see prices grind back and forth in a congestion zone. We could give the pattern a number of different names, but for the moment we will call it just a zone of contest between buyers and sellers. When the price breaks definitively below the lows of this zone the lower reaches (indeed all of it) become a resistance level. When prices return to this level we will expect to see a supply of stock become available and constitute resistance.

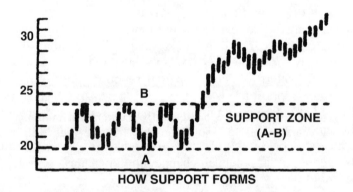

Diagram 2.   How Support Forms. As in Diagram 1, prices have been in a congestion zone but have broken out on the upside. If and when reactions occur there is the normal expectation that buying support will appear at the top of the zone to prop up prices. These are the buyers who "missed the boat on the breakout" and are glad to have a second chance to get on board.

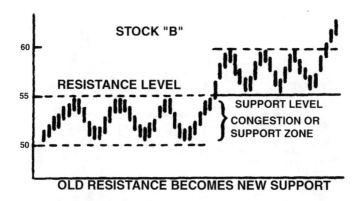

Diagram 3. Old Resistance Becomes New Support. A resistance zone once over-come becomes a source of future support. Here we see how the resistance zone has offered a line of support to higher prices once overcome.

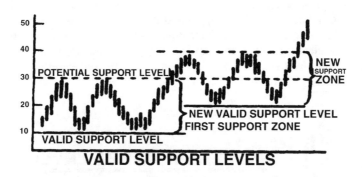

Diagram 4. Valid Support Levels. The top of a congestion zone will often serve as a support zone when prices have broken out, but other valid levels may develop, identifiable by volume behavior and the containment of prices within rational boundaries.

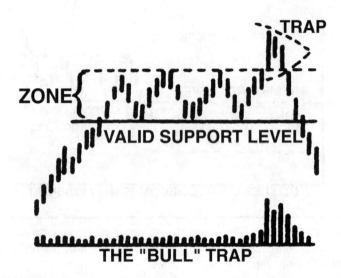

THE "BULL" TRAP

Diagram 5. The Bull Trap. When prices break out of a congestion or trading zone on the upside, even on good volume and conditions, bulls will rush to buy. When further action nullifies the signal and the price drops through what previously looked like support, we say that a "bull trap" has been sprung. Quite often the trade that develops after the trap is sprung turns out to be profitable (i.e., the trade on the short side). In fact, Schwager calls this subsequent signal one of the most reliable of pattern trades.

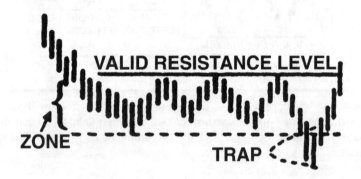

THE "BEAR" TRAP

Diagram 6. The Bear Trap. As in Diagram 5, the initial breakout, this time on the downside, is a feint, trapping bears who jump too fast. The subsequent trade, after the signal is canceled, can develop quite well.

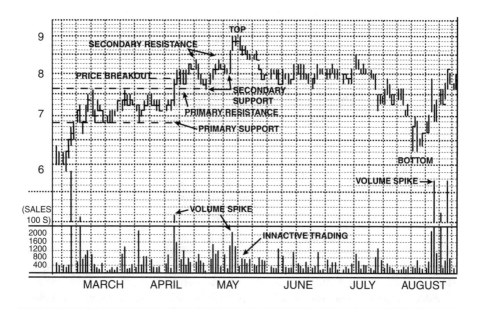

Diagram 7. Decoding a Bar Chart. Now we may look at the foregoing diagram with some understanding and identify zones of resistance and support, of price breakout, of tops and sell-offs. This chart is EveryMan's EveryStock. Here we have some support and resistance and some rectangles or battle zones and some tops and bottoms. In fine, EveryStock. Primary support and resistance develop along the horizontal trend lines of the rectangle. When price breaks out and encounters secondary resistance, it returns to the top of the rectangle and finds there the secondary support we expect to build up in normal times out of a zone such as this. After the top, the secondary support line holds the price up until those holders become discouraged after their second attempt at a breakout in July. And then sellers drive the price lower to the bottom. These are discouraged bulls. Notice the low volume on the downtrend. These fair-weather friends being out of the way, true believers can take control of the stock in August, driving it back up and causing acid indigestion in those who (probably rightly) sold out. Our cunning technical analysts bailed out in July (perhaps even going short) and bailed back in when the downtrend line was broken on eye-catching volume. *See* Diagram 1, How Resistance Forms.

Diagram 8.   Kilroy Bottom, Diagram of a More Persuasive Pattern to Rename Head-and-Shoulders Bottom. As may easily be seen in this amusing World War II graffito, the term "head-and-shoulders bottom" is innately disturbing. Much more logical and descriptive to call it what it is, a Kilroy bottom. In fact, there is much more accuracy in the nomenclature as complex formations might be said to have multiple fingers instead of multiple shoulders (of which the human model only has one of the left, etc.). The correspondence is obvious but I will gild the lily. Left hand equals left (upside down) shoulder. Nose equals (upside down) head. Right hand equals (upside down) right shoulder. Doesn't that make more sense than calling it an upside down head-and-shoulders bottom?

3

THE CENTRAL CONCEPT: THE IMPORTANCE OF TRENDS AND TREND CHANNELS

TRENDS

It almost always surprises novices to discover that on logarithmic charts the price moves so frequently lie along straight lines, forming "trend channels" that may run for months, or years. For example, the long-term uptrend in International Business Machines ran from the end of 1953 to the beginning of 1962 (*see Chart 6*), over 8 years, in one straight trend channel so precise you could lay a steel ruler along it and it would not violate the upward sloping trends at any point. Incidentally, when it did break this trend, in January 1962, the price dropped precipitously from over 600 to 300 in less than 6 months (*see Chart 10*). The trends of stocks normally move down faster than they move up.

It is easy to verify the existence of these straight-line trends. It is easy to see that stocks do not ordinarily jump around in completely random fluctuations but move in more or less orderly progression for considerable periods. However, knowing this does not automatically, and by itself, solve all problems. As a matter of fact, though it is worth knowing, it solves no problems. Before one can buy or sell a stock, it is necessary to have some clear idea of what constitutes a change in the trend, so that as far as possible one will not linger on the wrong side of the major trend. This is a matter calling for the most intense observation and study. It may require auxiliary studies. (For example, the volume of trading times the price of a stock represents the number of dollars involved in the market action on a particular day. It makes a great difference whether the total trading amounted to $10,000 or $10 million.) As we said before,

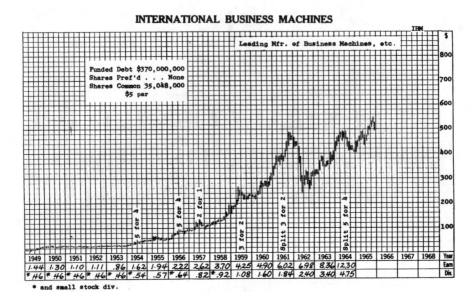

INTERNATIONAL BUSINESS MACHINES

Chart 6. IBM. Straight Trend from 1953 to 1962 and subsequent recovery. Courtesy of M.C. Horsey & Co. Inc. With permission.

the chart is merely a tool, a means of setting down graphically some data about the market action.

HINDSIGHT AS A WORKING TOOL

Many investors and traders focus on what is going on now in the market — not only in the market but as to corporate affairs, national politics, international affairs, monetary conditions, and so on. They are trying to interpret the present and estimate the probable future, but they are not well prepared to do this unless and until they have acquired some knowledge of the past. One of the most valuable study aids a technician can have is his file of stock charts for previous years. By studying how stocks have acted in the past, the typical action during booms and busts, the bottom formations and top patterns, the extent and duration of trends, and so on, he will be better prepared to evaluate a new situation. In fact, his intuition, his understanding of the market (which is in his mind, not in the chart), will develop as he acquires more experience, more understanding of what has happened in the past. The times may be different, the conditions may be different, the particular stock may be different from others that have been studied. And yet, although history does not exactly repeat itself, one learns what seems most likely to happen under certain circumstances.

This is like learning in any field. The surgeon, the lawyer, the musician, and the executive must continually face new problems not precisely like any encountered before. But they must have had the experience of analyzing other problems from the past that are in some significant ways similar. Thus, when the technician is confronted with an entirely new problem, he can draw on this storehouse of experience and, by "playing it by ear," put to use the intuitive knowledge he has gained from these past events.

We cannot make the point too strongly that chart interpretation and technical market wisdom is not learned overnight. We cannot stress too much the importance of looking back, and if the technician has noted his past opinions and evaluations on the charts (as he should, to get the most value from them), of checking these out and seeing where his judgments were good, where they failed, and, if they failed, whether it seemed to be because of some correctable error in judgment or whether it was because of an unexpected and unpredictable change of conditions.

TRENDS, REVERSALS, CORRECTIONS, AND CONSOLIDATIONS

If we agree that the chart is a valid representation of the daily price and volume action in the market, and if we agree that it is primarily the market that makes the charts go and not the chart that makes the market go, we can regard the chart as a map of conditions that exist in the market.

As long as we keep it clearly in mind that our map, though accurate and correct in what it shows, does not show everything (no map shows everything in the territory it represents), we can deal with the chart (or map) in many ways as if it were the territory itself.

We will look for relations, but we must be careful not to attribute causes too freely. Quite often it is not necessary or possible to know the cause or causes of a market condition, even though we know very well that there must be causes. It can be dangerous to pin causes on things. If, for example, we were to say the birds return in the spring and the leaves get green in the spring, then the leaves get green because the birds come back, we would be quite wrong. And we might dangerously confuse ourselves in giving weight to a cause-and-effect relationship between drug addicts and inferior abilities. One might assume that because inferior behavior and drug addiction are frequently found in association, the drug addiction was the cause or reason for the inferior behavior in work, social relations, and so on. Or, vice versa, we might assume that general incompetence and inferior abilities were the cause of addiction. This might indeed be a false lead that could confuse understanding of the problem. Better to treat relationships simply as relationships, without continually trying to pin a cause-and-effect label on the relations.

If we can take the chart as an abstraction, leaving causes and effects out of it, we can see some relations that might otherwise be overlooked.

For example, the chart of a utility stock may show a definite technical pattern, let us say a rectangular horizontal channel from which the price breaks away sharply upward or downward on increased volume. We may, in fact we do, see other charts with almost identical patterns and behavior — steel stocks, oil stocks, motors, rubbers, and so on. In fact, this particular type of market pattern may turn up in any type of stock at some time or other; for that matter, it may appear in bond charts, commodity charts, or in the charts of anything traded in a free competitive market (*see Chart 7*).

The Constant Recurrence of Similar Patterns

Because the same type of pattern, with the same sort of breakout and similar consequences after the breakout, shows up again and again in many different kinds of market charts, we must conclude that the chart pattern is not a particular characteristic of railroads or steel companies, for example, but is more likely related to the dynamics of markets generally or, to be more specific, to the perceptive habits of people. In a sense, we are looking much more at the operation of men's minds than at the conditions affecting a corporation. Or, shall we say, if we are looking at the affairs of the corporation, we are seeing them "as perceived" by the buyers and sellers in the market, and it is that perception and evaluation that are recorded on the chart. The underlying reasons could be many. It is not actually necessary to inquire in detail what they are.

Again, we find the same trends and chart patterns on charts representing market action in *2001 as those of 1979, or 1929, or 1889 (see Chart 8 for the tops of three historic bull markets)*. An experienced technical trader today could be taken back in time 30 years; he could be confronted with stocks in a foreign market, and, if he were familiar with the typical behavior of stocks generally, as it is shown on the daily charts, he could draw some useful information from the charts. He might even operate better in such an unfamiliar market than some who are so close to it they "could not see the forest for the trees."

Let us consider a stock that has been selling in a dull sort of way, for a considerable time, at or near a certain price range. Suddenly, it comes to life. It advances sharply and on much increased volume. It is possible that such a breakout may come about through a false rumor, a piece of gossip about the stock, or perhaps a premature "guess" that something is about to happen. If the trader felt that there was a good chance that such-and-such a company would get the big aircraft contract next month, or might be merged on favorable terms with one of its competitors, or was about to win an important lawsuit, he might well buy some of the stock,

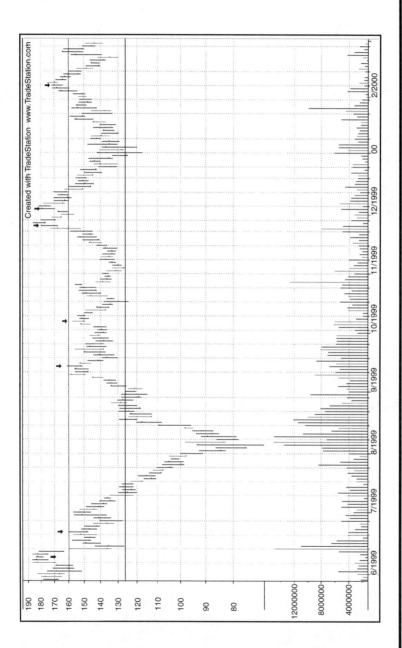

Chart 7. Ebay, Largely Horizontal at this Moment in Time. The sideways channel is probably as common as, or perhaps even more common than, uptrend or downtrend channels. Here once again illustrating support and resistance, and also the failure of support, Ebay also offers good short-term trading opportunities. It is a common technique for traders to sell the top of a trading range or horizontal channel and buy the bottom. In this chart the arrows illustrate this technique, taking key reversal days as the signal. The August volume is probably mutual fund managers running for the exits. At the least it is unhappy bulls helping to create a bottom.

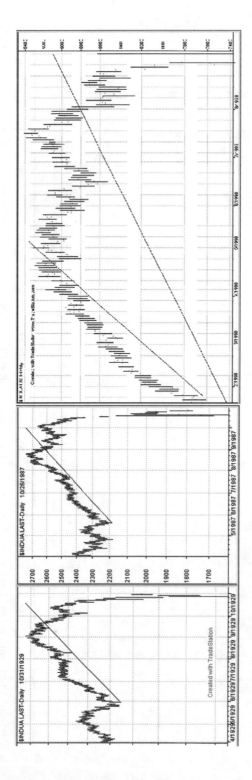

Chart 8. Dow-Jones Industrials. Three Bull Market Tops: 1929, 1987, 1998. The reader will note the common element to all these bull market tops: an important trendline has been broken. Continuing price action under the trendline (especially in Magee's opinion if by 2% in the case of the Dow) is an escalating warning. An investor might be justified in setting his stop line at or under the forming rectangle or pattern if the market were not of such long duration — but at the end of bull markets of these durations extreme caution is a sign of market wisdom, not paranoia or cowardice. At the very least hedging is in order.

and if some others felt as he did, they might well be willing to pay a little more than the market price to get their shares. If there were enough eager buyers, this could use up all the available stock offered at the prices at which this stock had been selling and eventually force the bids considerably higher in order to attract sellers willing to part with some of their holdings.

Whether or not a particular breakout of this sort will be the beginning of a long and profitable advance depends on whether the original information was correct and whether the expected action takes place and other factors. But, when a big move in a stock does take place, it is likely to emerge from just this kind of situation. If the trader is not too impetuous, does not jump in too heavily and risk too much, and if he is prepared to get out again, often with a loss in case the move fails, he is likely to pick up one of the important instances in which a new major trend is getting under way.

No One Ever Went Broke Taking a Profit. True or False?

However, it is all too common for an inexperienced trader to become nervous as his stock advances. Sometimes it seems he will suffer more when a stock is going his way than when it is moving against him. There seems to be a temptation to get out too soon, to "take profits," and, in fact, one of the oldest (and most misleading) market maxims is, "No man ever went broke taking a profit." Although the statement is true, the implications of it are deceptive, for unless a man can stick with a strong stock as long as it remains strong, his losses may outweigh his gains.

It is best not to be too urgently anxious to get out of a profitable stock. Checking the records of some dozens or hundreds of stocks, as shown on long-term monthly charts, we find that the major trends do not switch from strong to weak and weak to strong every week or so. We will see plainly that usually a well-established trend in a stock continues for some time, that is, for months, sometimes for years. The upmoving stock is likely to continue to move up. The downmoving stock continues to slide.

Therefore, once we have determined or decided that a stock is in a major trend, if we have a position in that stock in line with the trend, we should stay with it until there is some evidence that the stock is no longer moving in that trend.

A Method Is Required to Avoid Premature Profit Taking

This is easier said than done, of course, because every stock has its daily fluctuations and is also subject to the general dips and rallies of the market as a whole. Nevertheless, it is possible to make some observations, to set up some rules of procedure, and, in time, to acquire a "method" based on observation and experience which will help in getting into stocks in line with their major trends and in getting out of these positions only when the trend seems seriously threatened. Not only will the investor acquire a set of principles or rules of operation, but, more important, he will gradually get a feeling or intuition of the action of stocks as a result of having followed, observed, and tentatively judged many such actions in the past.

It is not possible to make a simple set of maxims or directives that can be used as a formula and that will absolutely prevent loss and ensure profits. The market is not that easy. Furthermore, each investor has his own objectives and philosophy. Some are interested only in short-term gains; they are temperamental in-and-outers and do not feel at ease in a long-time holding. If they understand clearly that the problems of the short-time market trader are complicated by high costs to cover the frequent commissions, transfer taxes, miscellaneous fees, and unavoidable execution losses, and if they are prepared for the nerve-wracking, tense battle all day and every day, they may be able to hold their own in that small group of short-term traders who are successful on balance.

For most of us, the more profitable course lies in holding a stock position as long as it looks good and closing it out just as soon as it no longer seems tenable. This also requires courage and constant study, and, in addition, it requires the most difficult quality of all — the ability to sit and wait, sometimes for weeks or months. It calls for patience.

Whether the plan is short-term trading or long-term, the investor must be prepared to accept losses, to forget what he paid for the stock, and to deal with it according to its current action only, regardless of whether it shows him an accrued gain or loss at a given time.

CHANGES IN TREND CALL FOR CHANGES OF POSITION

Suppose we have taken a long position in a stock which has broken out of dormancy, as we described previously. We will assume that the stock has entered a major uptrend, and this trend will be considered in effect until such time as there are indications that convince us that the trend has been broken decisively.

This, of course, is easy to say and much harder to do. The whole science or art of technical analysis of stock trends is involved here, and it depends a great deal on the individual skill, experience, and perception of the investor as to how well he will do. It also depends on whether he has the conviction and courage to follow and carry out with determination the decisions his method lead to.

Finally, it calls for a realistic understanding that in spite of the most careful, most intelligent study of a stock situation, there is still a consid-erable area of uncertainty. No one can make predictions with anything

Chart 9. Microsoft. How a Historic Bull Market Ended. At the top of the Microsoft bull market is a fine rectangle that advertises itself as a consolidation, especially with the runaway days on breakout. But the short cap after the runaways and the return to their base are ominous signs. Beneath the surface the general bull market is ending, and Microsoft is locked in a death struggle with the Justice Department and assumes that like all its other struggles it will prevail here also. As a further sign that its day in the sun is done (for the moment), the Dow-Jones Company adds Microsoft to the Dow-Jones Industrials. Spectacularly bad timing for all involved. No technical analyst would have held the stock in spite of its long glorious record when the medium and then the long-term trend lines were broken. That is what technical analysis is for, to make obvious the unbelievable, that Microsoft could fall. All stocks eventually suffer intermediate- or long-term decline. Nothing lasts forever.

like absolute certainty. If the investor is satisfied his method and original basis of decision were correct, if the situation changes greatly, he must be prepared to face the fact that some new conditions have arisen, and he must act accordingly. It is no reflection on his method that he should have to revise his opinion or reverse his decision in light of new facts. One of the most damaging, sometimes ruinous, points of view is that of the man who is so "wedded" to his original conclusion that he cannot face the fact that the situation is different this month from what it may have been 3 months ago.

FOLLOWING THE TREND

There are almost as many definitions of a trend as there are investors to make them. Normally, the trend of a stock is a more or less irregular affair, with bursts of high volume as new peaks are reached and then periods of a few days or a few weeks with shrinking volume of trading, followed by another advance on increasing volume. Some setbacks may be short and of limited extent — a few days or a week, perhaps. Others, especially after a series of minor advances, may be of greater extent and may last for a number of weeks or several months. Yet all these may fit into the category of major uptrend.

No method of determining whether or not the major trend is still in effect is infallible. However, there are a number of methods of estimating whether or not an important change of trend has occurred.

The simplest of these is to draw a trendline — that is, a line which touches the bottoms of two or more reactions if the major trend is up (*see Diagram 9*). (In the case of downmoving stocks, the trendline would be drawn across the tops of two or more rallies.) In many cases the trend follows a straight line, especially on logarithmically scaled charts, and a sharp breakdown through the trendline dramatically underscores the change of the trend.

A case in point would be the long-term trend in International Business Machines (IBM). After more than 8 years of following a perfectly straight trendline, IBM broke through that line in January 1962 and by the end of May had dropped several hundred points. However, after that 1962 correction, IBM resumed the long-term trendline through 1989 (*see Chart 10*).

In spite of the clear evidence that trends do exist and that they follow straight lines on logarithmic charts, the simple trendline is not by any means the whole answer to stock analysis — far from it. It is not always easy or possible to find clear points of reference through which to draw the trendline. Quite frequently, the chart shows a sideways movement that will penetrate the trendline without volume or any substantial decline. It is necessary to understand that the way in which the trendline is broken may be as important as, or more important than, the fact it is broken (*see Chart 11*).

Alternatives to the Simple Trendline

To get around the difficulties of dealing with simple trendlines, various refinements and alternatives have been developed. Some technicians require a breakdown that penetrates the line by a definite minimum amount, say 3% or 5% of the price of the stock. Others use double trendlines, forming a channel that includes a warning area between a slight penetration and a full-scale signal. Some use, instead of the ordinary trendline, a moving average, which may be based on the performance over any preceding period; we have 10-day moving averages, 30-day moving averages, 100-day and 200-day moving averages, and so on. This

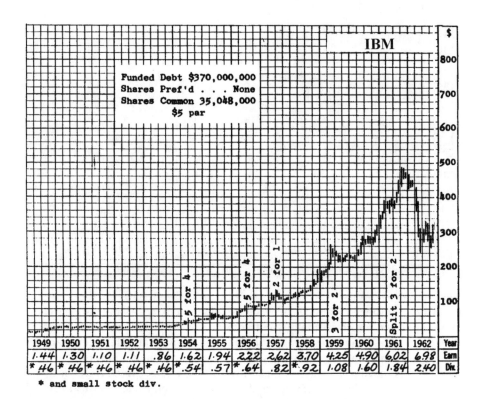

Chart 10.   IBM. January 1962, End of Another Historic Bull Market. Courtesy of M.C. Horsey & Co. Inc. With permission.

tends to stabilize the picture and eliminate certain types of false or trivial moves, but it also introduces some other problems peculiar to moving averages. There have been methods in which two moving averages, a short-term and a longer-term one, are used together to give indications of change of trend when they cross (*see Chart 35*). There are a number of other methods using trendlines, moving averages, and some other devices to catch early signs of a major turn.

Although none of these methods is entirely satisfactory, any of them is better than no method at all. They may not catch the exact or optimum point at which a decision could best be made, but they will at least ensure that an investor who follows them will not allow himself indefinitely to hold a stock that is piling up losses for him after a major reversal.

There are other indications of turn and some suggest a continuation of the major trend. The latter we have called consolidation patterns. The former we call reversal patterns.

Chart 11. **Advanced Micro Devices, Inc. Stocks tend to make straight-line trends, either up, down, or horizontally. The trends do not necessarily move in the same direction as "the Dow Jones Average" or "the general market." Here, for example, we see a strong downtrend in a particular stock at a time when the "general market" was moving sideways to higher. From June to December, AMD declined by nearly 50% in the face of a generally bullish market. Although this issue did enjoy a rally back to 11 during the first half of 1989, the downtrend resumed the following June while the "averages" were challenging old highs. You will find some issues moving sharply higher in bear markets and others, like AMD, moving down in bull markets. This type of action does not strike us as "random." Apparently, some economic or psychological factors were operating to affect public opinion. But it is not necessary for the market technician to know what these factors may have been. The chart speaks for itself.**

Behavior at the End of Trends

In many cases, the consolidation patterns in their early stages look exactly like the reversal patterns in their early stages (*see Chart 12*). In fact, they probably arise from the same cause. When a stock has advanced in a strongly bullish move for a time (or declined in a bearish move), there will come a day when traders decide to take profits (if they are on the right side of the stock), and what frequently occurs after a rapid price move is a great increase of activity culminating in a burst of tremendously increased volume.

In the final day of a fast advance, the price may open on a "gap," higher than the top price of the day before, and may go into entirely new high ground in the morning but then slump off as the day wears on, closing

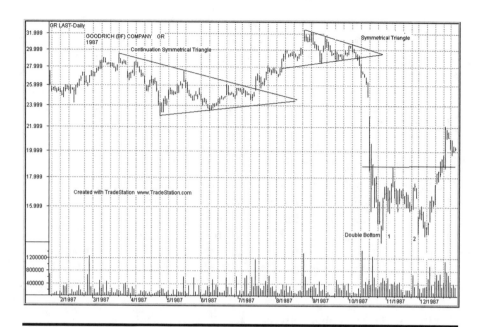

Chart 12. B.F. Goodrich Company. Not only can chart patterns be described in several ways, many can be either reversal or continuation patterns. The Goodrich chart shows two unusually good examples, quite close together, of the dual nature of some chart patterns. After moving steadily higher in 1986 and early 1987, this issue turned sideways. From April through July, we see a series of advances and declines which all together add up to a narrowing symmetrical triangle. In mid-July, on sharply higher volume, Goodrich broke out of the pattern to resume its previous uptrend. Using the width of the pattern as a measure, you would have anticipated a move to the 63 area and not been disappointed when Goodrich peaked in early September around 64½. This is a symmetrical triangle as a continuation pattern. Following the September peak, another series of fluctuations emerged, also taking the shape of a symmetrical triangle. This time the decisive breakout was contra to the prevailing uptrend, illustrating a reversal symmetrical triangle. Notice the excellent double bottom that formed on the December test of the October low. The late December rally through 37, on rising volume, was a clear signal that the downtrend was over. During the next two years, Goodrich rallied to 70.

at or near the low for the day's trading. Such a climax day or one-day reversal is quite commonly the peak, the end of the advance for the time being. Following it, there may be a few days, a week or so, or a number of weeks, of decline or at least of inconsequential sideways movement, and this period is usually marked by irregularly shrinking volume.

Whether or not the one-day reversal will prove to be of more than minor importance or not, we cannot tell at this stage, although many high-water marks preceding a severe Bear Market have been made on exactly this sort of day.

What seems more important here is that the one-day reversal, or, at any rate, a climax day of high volume, quite often marks the end of one phase of an advance.

Corrections and Consolidations Occur Frequently

In any stock that is moving up (and what we say here would apply in reverse for downmoving stocks, of course), there are likely to be fairly frequent periods of correction or consolidation, not necessarily, however, marking the ultimate end of the major trend (*see Chart 13*).

A common type of consolidation occurs when the stock goes into a narrow horizontal range, moving, for example, from 32 to 36, and fluctuating back and forth within these limits in moves that may last a few days to a week or so. Ordinarily, as this rectangle forms on the chart, the volume tends to shrink, although in a bullish trend, the peaks of the rallies may be marked by somewhat increased volume. In time, the stock will emerge from the rectangle, and if this is an upside breakout, it will almost certainly be on greatly increased volume and will be quite unmistakable. Such a breakout suggests that (1) the major uptrend is still in effect and that further advances are probable, and (2) there is likely to be an influx of support (buying) on any reaction to the neighborhood of the top of the rectangle. In a major downtrend we also see rectangles with similar characteristics except that volume on the downside moves or breakouts may not be so emphatically marked.

Rectangles (*see Diagram 13 and Chart 13*) are among the most beautiful and most interesting of the technical formations that appear on charts. They may be either consolidations (or continuation patterns) or the mark of an important turn (reversal pattern). During their formation, it is not possible to say whether they mark a consolidation or a reversal, but, on the basis that a major trend must be assumed to be in effect until there is clear evidence of reversal, the presumption is that they are consolidations until there is a contrary breakout. As a matter of fact, the majority of rectangles, symmetrical triangles, and so on do turn out to be consolidations.

A good example of a rectangle as shown on a chart is to be seen in the 1988–1989 BankAmerica chart (*see Chart 13*). The Glossary of Patterns includes a conceptual diagram.

One could regard rectangles as "horizontal trend channels," with tentative trendlines drawn across the tops and bottoms.

Chart 13. Bankamerica Corporation. There are those who will tell us that the movements of stocks are as completely random as the stumblings of a drunk in a public square late at night, or as meaningless as the scores of a blindfolded dart player. Anyone who has kept daily charts of stocks knows that the charts do not provide "all the answers," nor do they infallibly "predict the future." But it is hard to believe that the trends such as the uptrend shown here in BankAmerica or the uptrend and downtrend in Advanced Micro Devices could be the result of the gyrations of a drunk or the scores of a blindfolded dart player. In the Bank-America chart you will also notice two other typical patterns, the falling wedge and rectangle. The first is considered a bullish pattern, and confirmation is given when the upper boundary line is decisively broken on increasing volume. Rect-angles, on the other hand, can be continuation or reversal patterns, depending on which way they break out of the formation. Generally speaking, rectangles define a tug of war between two groups of approximately equal strength. The stock will bounce back and forth, trading within two horizontal boundary lines, until one side or the other is exhausted. The measuring implication of this pattern (i.e., the expected minimum movement after the breakout) is the width of the rectangle. A rectangle 2 points wide, for example, should move at least 2 points beyond its breakout point.

When a breakout from such a pattern occurs, it is quite common to see the move run a few days and then return to approximately the breakout level before resuming the primary move.

This raises the interesting point of support and resistance phenomena. When a stock has made a dynamic breakout move, this move is likely to

QUALCOM (58.7500,62.0625, 58.0000, 59.8750, +1.5625)

Created with MetaStock www.equis.com

Chart 14. Qualcomm, Symmetrical Triangles. The handwriting is already on the wall for Qualcomm when this symmetrical triangle appears in its chart, perhaps bringing a moment of hope to bulls that it might be a continuation pattern. But the church spire top and the air pocket gap formed at the beginning of the triangle have already forecast its fate. Would the long trader be justified in holding out for the second cruel joke, the false upside breakout? No. All the trendlines are pointing the wrong way. Denial is not just a river in Egypt. It is also refusing to recognize the end of the party, the passing of all good things, the boats beating backward against the current, the end of the millennium, etc.

be followed by some quick profit taking, and a reaction sets in. However, many observers believe that prospective buyers who may have missed the original breakout may then come into the market on the reaction. It is this buying that constitutes the support that so frequently appears at or near the bottoms of rectangles (or in bearish moves, the resistance that appears at or near the bottom of rectangles).

There is another type of market action that is somewhat similar to the rectangle. This type has the form of a more or less symmetrical triangle, and we call it by that name (*see Chart 14*).

It is marked, usually, by a heavy volume climax as it goes into its first turning point, which is followed by a series of declines and rallies that, instead of forming two parallel lines, as is the case of the rectangles, tend to narrow, so that the lines drawn across the turning points make a downsloping and upsloping side to the triangle. It is a "narrowing" formation, ordinarily accompanied by shrinking volume. The triangle may eventually turn into a rectangle. More often it breaks out decisively at some point well before it reaches the apex or intersection of its two bounding trendlines. The symmetrical triangles often mark important consolidations and sometimes important reversals. They are more subject to false moves than are rectangles, as when the price makes an "end run" entirely around the apex of the triangle and reverses the move entirely. An interesting feature of the symmetrical triangle is the market tendency of reactions after an emphatic breakout to return to the point of intersection of the two sides of the triangle — the "cradle point" as Robert D. Edwards has called it.

Uncertainty of Direction of Breakouts from Rectangles and Triangles

With both the rectangles and symmetrical triangles there is little indication of which way the breakout will occur. There is, however, another family of triangles that carries a definite indication of the probable move to come. These triangles are known as ascending triangles (in which the successive minor peaks are at substantially the same price level and the successive bottoms are at continually higher levels) and descending triangles (in which the minor bottoms come at about the same price level but successive rallies top out at continually lower levels) (*see Charts 15 and 16*).

The ascending triangle (*see Chart 16*) apparently corresponds to a resistance level (or supply level), and the successively rising bottoms show the tendency of investors to be willing to pay more for the stock on its declines. The reverse would be true of the descending triangle (*see Chart 15*). Thus, these types of triangle patterns can generally be regarded as bullish (for the ascending type) and normally bearish (for the descending type). In some cases, these patterns, like all chart patterns, fail, and even when they do not completely fail they are often prone to turning into rectangles as time goes on. But all in all, the ascending and descending triangles are among the most dependable of chart patterns.

Measuring Price Moves — Or Estimating Potential Price Activity

The question of measurement is bound to come up in connection with chart formations. It is not possible to make very accurate estimates as to how far a move will go. At best, one can state a minimum probable move, but we would not consider that a stock that has made such a minimum probable move and has reached its estimated objective should be sold. If the move is part of a major trend, the advance may continue far beyond the objective and there is no guarantee, in any case, that a particular target will be reached. We would use any measuring formulas as guides or auxiliary information, but we would not hold to them as to a religion.

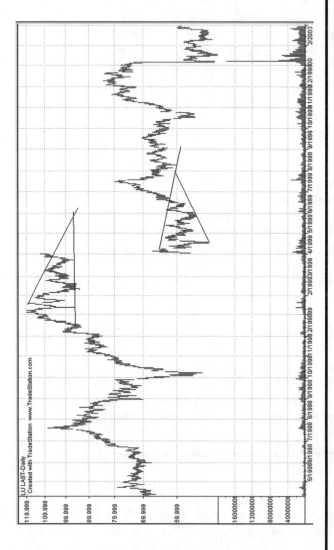

Chart 15. Lucent, Descending Triangle. This top of Lucent is marked by a particularly vicious descending triangle, particularly vicious because it contains a false breakout, a bull trap which would have left the impatient or inexperienced bull long just in time for the air pocket and given him firsthand experience with catastrophic risk. Lucent is, of course, psychotic. But at least it makes a bottom after the plunge in the form of a symmetrical triangle, which is tradable but which, when it returns to the cradle of the triangle, is offering a hint to the wise: go find another stock to trade. Was crashing with the stock a necessity? Not really. A 3-month trendline was decisively broken well before the plunge, and the use of the basing-points procedure would also have taken out a systematic technician. Perhaps an even more elemental procedure would have avoided the whole situation in the first place — that is, the careful choice of stocks that make up the portfolio. On the other hand, the bungee trader using very sensitive tactics might be delighted with Lucent.

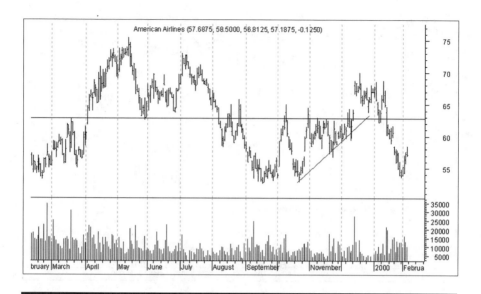

Chart 16. American Airlines, Ascending Triangle. Making an ascending triangle against a resistance line American Airlines makes a good breakaway gap through the top boundary of the triangle, but late in development of the pattern, and with no follow-through. A key reversal day follows a few days later, the gap is closed, and the handwriting is on the wall. Given that the entire range from 63 to 70 is a heavy resistance zone, it is not surprising that the breakaway is a bull trap. Once again the observation that a failed signal on one side is a good signal on the other is demonstrated, but there is probably an even more fundamental question about American Airlines to begin with — namely, does it have enough up and down range to be a good investment vehicle? Investment vehicle in the sense that is there a likelihood of long fruitful trends?

In general, we assume that the probable move out of a pattern, such as the rectangles, symmetrical triangles, and ascending and descending triangles will be at least equal to the measurement of the pattern on its first "leg." In the case of the rectangles, this would mean the measurement from top to bottom. With the triangles, it would be the same distance as the "open side" of the triangle.

Flags and Pennants and Their Implications

There is another type of continuation pattern that should be mentioned here. Generally, it is a consolidation or continuation pattern, and it is frequently found in the charts of stocks that are making a large and rapid move either up or down. We will speak here of the upmoving case, but the downmoving is quite similar, in reverse.

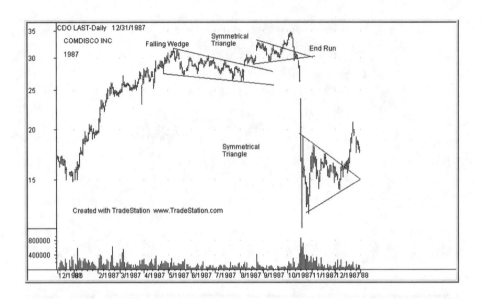

Chart 17. Comdisco, Inc. It is not always possible to make an "overperfect" picture of a technical situation. There may be premature and/or false breakouts to cloud the picture. End runs are also a hazard. This, of course, is why we employ stop-loss protection. Here, we see several examples of false breakouts, and an end run, on the same chart. Beginning in April, CDO began to fluctuate sideways in a narrowing but slightly downward-slanting pattern. Initially, several formations were possible. But, as the consolidation stretched out into July, it took the shape of a falling wedge. This is a bullish pattern, so an upside breakout would be expected. Notice that in late July, however, support was broken. This would have called for some special attention, but it did not go far outside the boundary of the wedge before pulling back into the formation. It happened in early August as well, but, again, the break was not decisive and the close in both cases was basically on the boundary line. These two breakouts were false. The true breakout came shortly thereafter on a high-volume rally through the upper boundary line. CDO turned sideways again, forming an excellent symmetrical triangle on diminishing volume. In late September, it broke out of the triangle on the upside. The rally stalled a week later, and prices plunged back through triangle support on heavy volume, a clear failure of the breakout which "has aptly been termed an end run around the line." CDO formed a large symmetrical triangle after the crash and broke to the upside in early December, retracing most of its October loss over the next 2 years.

The patterns we are speaking of occur after a rapid, almost vertical advance, oftentimes a move that may "gap" from day to day and which may cover many points in a week or in 2 weeks' time. There may be a one-day reversal at the end of such a "leg" in a move, or there may not. But the stock is quite likely, in any case, to "stall," to decline, and then,

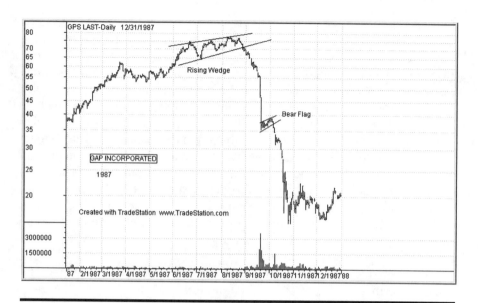

Chart 18. Gap, Inc. GPS was a spectacular performer in the decade of the 1980s. From under 1 in 1980, this issue exceeded 76 at its 1987 peak. Along the way, it also suffered some substantial setbacks. To look at a long-term chart (monthly), these downturns look as if they materialized out of thin air. Although it is true that stocks can reverse dramatically when some sort of fundamental news hits everyone by surprise, like a particularly disguised takeover attempt, or a disaster like the gas leak in Bhopal, India, which hurt Union Carbide, more often than not, signs of a change of direction will show up in the daily chart. In GPS, for example, it was hard to miss the deteriorating technical position which occurred through the summer of 1987. Oscillating higher, on generally weakening volume, (note that each high from June on occurred on lower volume), GPS formed a fine rising wedge pattern. Just opposite of the falling wedge (see Comdisco chart), this pattern has bearish implications. Well before the rest of the market collapsed, Comdisco (CDO) had fallen through support and was heading sharply lower. An excellent bear flag, evident at the end of September, was also completed before the October crash in the general market.

with volume shrinking sharply, to go into a tight, narrow pattern as seen on the chart, such as a flag or pennant which may be flying horizontally or may be drooping somewhat. If anyone seeks an explanation of this sudden halt and consolidation, he may well regard this as a period of profit taking by quick-turn speculators or the rather premature selling out of investors who are overeager to take profits. It will, undoubtedly, represent, too, the trading of those who hope to sell the stock near a temporary top and then buy in on the first reaction (*see Chart 18*).

In any case, such a pattern is not to be regarded as bearish. It normally suggests the likelihood of a powerful resumption of the move in the near future. Although, as with all market phenomena, this is not a certainty, the rewards of patience during the flag-and-pennant-type corrections are often richly worth exercising that patience.

Schabacker has stated that flags and pennants carry a rather definite measuring implication, namely, that the continuation of the move after a breakout from the flag or pennant is likely to measure about as much as the original fast move leading into the pattern, or, as he put it, "The flag flies at half-mast." It is extraordinary how often this particular measurement is completed. But, in such a case, we would not feel that after the attainment of the objective the stock should be sold. For it can go into another continuation pattern and then break out again for still further advances.

There are a number of other technical patterns, trend actions, support and resistance phenomena, and so on, which might be studied but would require an entire book to deal with adequately. (In fact, see *Technical Analysis of Stock Trends*, 8th ed.)

However, there is one particular chart picture that is of such prime importance that we have saved discussion of it for the last.

This is the head-and-shoulders pattern which can appear at both tops and bottoms, and which is a major indication of reversal, which has appeared in the charts of dozens or hundreds of stocks during every important market top or bottom (*see Chart 20*).

This pattern was observed and discussed in connection with stock averages by Charles H. Dow and William Peter Hamilton over half a century ago. It was studied extensively by Richard W. Schabacker and was explained in considerable detail by Rollo Tape (alias Richard Wyckoff) in his fine book, *Studies in Tape Reading* in 1910.

The head-and-shoulders top (*see Diagram 23*) in its simplest form consists of the next-to-last and the final rallies in a major uptrend, the first (failing) rally of a major downtrend, and the penetration of the "neckline" marking the bottoms between the rallies.

Typically, a stock, and often an average, follows a major trend in a series of waves (i.e., advances interrupted by corrective reactions). This movement has been compared to the advance of the incoming tide on a beach, not steadily but in a series of advancing high-water points as the breakers wash higher and higher up the sands. When the succession of large waves begins to fall short of a high-water mark, and the intervening ebb runs back to a lower point, one can infer that "the tide has turned." It is a good analogy.

The head-and-shoulders top is normally marked, like most technical patterns, by unusually high volume on the "left shoulder." The "head," which goes to a new high on the price scale, will ordinarily have less volume accompanying it. The (lower) "right shoulder" is usually made on relatively lower volume.

Chart 19. Nike Kilroy (or as it is sometimes known, head-and-shoulders) Bottom.
The Kilroy bottom like its opposite number is marked by an effort to find a level unsuccessfully — that is, the left hand or shoulder and then another effort in the same direction which exhausts the power of that side. Buyers in the case of the head-and-shoulders top, sellers in the case of the Kilroy bottom. Retreating from the head (or nose) the sellers make one last attempt and then the other side begins to achieve dominance. As illustrated here, the pattern may be part of a larger bottom finding which is one reason that seeing the pattern as possessing fingers as well as hands, or shoulders, makes taxonomic sense. As in the chart reproduced here, the hands may be abrupt and of short duration. And the pattern may be of a complex sort which requires some analysis. The one thing which will be true is that among the various hands, fingers, and noses, there will be a definable neckline. Otherwise what is at first suspected to be a Kilroy bottom will peter out and become a long rectangle or other complex form.

The neckline of such a pattern appears to represent good support, and, until and unless it is broken, it is probably best not to try to jump the gun by assuming the head and shoulders will be completed by such a breakthrough. When a neckline breakdown happens, it may be on increased volume or it may not. However, such a break, even though it merely drifts through the neckline on small volume, should not be taken lightly. If it has substantially broken the neckline (say by 3% of the price of the stock), it is likely to indicate a serious situation.

After such a break, there may be a rally. Although there is no promise or certainty of such a rally, it does occur in many, and, perhaps, a majority of cases. But this rally usually gets no farther than the general level of

Chart 20. Dillard Department Stores Inc. This is a head-and-shoulders top. The head-and-shoulders patterns, top and bottom, are the most well-known of the classical charts; they are also the most reliable of the major reversal patterns. Here, the price action traces the head-and-shoulders very clearly, breaking away on the downside with an open gap. During what proved to be the 1987 peak in the "averages" in August and September, a significant number of individual stocks, such as DDS, were clearly showing topping activity. The actual breakdown in the stock market in October, therefore, was not surprising; only the speed and the depth of the collapse were. It should be noted, however, that stocks almost always go down faster than they go up. Except for takeover situations, you will make money quicker on the short side of the market than on the long side. Indeed, it took Dillard 4 months to drop from roughly 58 to 24; it took 17 months to recoup the loss. This head-and-shoulders top exhibits the typical volume characteristics of the pattern — higher trading volume on the left shoulder than the head, and relatively flat volume on the right shoulder. The penetration of the neckline showed higher volume but would also be valid on low volume as long as it were broken by 3%.

the neckline, and the dropoff from here is likely to be precipitous and on greater volume.

Measuring Implications of the Head and Shoulders

The question can be asked, "How much of a decline might one expect after a definite head-and-shoulders break?" The most that one can be fairly definite of expecting is a decline amounting to the height of the pattern itself; that is, the height from the top of the head to the neckline will represent the minimum expected drop from the point of penetration of the neckline.

The comment may well be made that this is not such a great drop, and that if this is all there is to it, it might be best to hold the stock or even buy it on the decline. This, however, is not the whole story. When a major uptrend has been in effect for a long time, say, 6 months or a year or more, and then a pattern of this sort appears, either a head-and-shoulders, a large descending triangle, or a long rectangle broken on the downside, it may indicate a change in the major trend. There is a presumption, or at least a suspicion, that the successive rallies will come lower and lower and that the stock may plunge in a series of drops that may far exceed the minimum implications of the original top formation. We would never disregard a clearly formed and definitely broken head-and-shoulders top or any other typical top pattern.

We have spoken about the simple head-and-shoulders top, but there are many minor variations of this pattern. There may be a double head; there may be two or more left shoulders at about the same height, or two or more right shoulders. In the case of slow-moving, large-issue investment stocks, this type of pattern may become a rounding top (*see Chart 21*), having few, if any, definite rallies and declines but with the general picture of heavy upside volume gradually petering out and then increasing again as the stock "rounds over" and starts its downtrend.

In the case of head-and-shoulders (*or Kilroy*) bottoms (*see Diagram 8 and Chart 19*), the situation is similar but reversed. The formation is "upside down" and some writers have referred to it as a pendant bottom. Here, we have the heavy volume on the left shoulder, a rally, then a further drop to a new low (the head), and a recovery move that is likely to be marked by somewhat more volume than we have seen on a rally for some time. A corrective reaction on low volume takes the stock part way down again (right shoulder), and then a sharp advance occurs (which must be on heavy volume), smashing through the neckline defined by the two previous minor rallies.

The main differences between the head-and-shoulders tops and bottoms are that (1) the top formations are often completed in a few weeks, whereas a major bottom of any sort usually takes longer, and, in some cases, may cover from several months to a year and a half; and (2) the breakout move from head-and-shoulders top formations may not be marked by much increase in volume, whereas, the breakout from the head-and-shoulders bottom must have volume confirmation.

In concluding this discussion of daily charts and their use, we would once more like to emphasize that the chart is merely a map of what the market is doing and the market action is a composite of what people are thinking about a stock or about the market. There is no magic to a chart

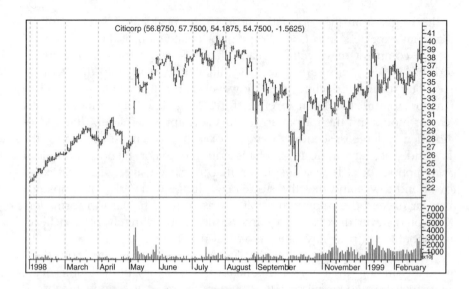

Chart 21. Citicorp, Rounding Top. In all likelihood the technician would have (or should have) been long before the breakaway gap and runaway gap in May. The rounding pattern does not become obvious until August, but what might be a neckline or a trendline constructed across the lows of the top should take the trader out before or around the gap. Basing-point stops would also have preserved the major part of profits. A short position might well have been established, in fact, especially on the symmetrical triangle from which prices plunge in September. Courtesy of Metastock, www.equis.com.

picture. It is a visual aid to the investor's thinking. In the final analysis, his success will depend in large part on his own powers of abstraction, observation, and ability to follow in practice the decisions he has arrived at in his mind. Continual study and review, backchecking on previous decisions and their consequences, experimentation and trial and error cannot help but build confidence, eliminate mistakes in trading, and improve one's practical ability to cope with the market.

TREND CHANNELS

At the start of this trend study, we applied the term "basic trendline" to the line that slopes up across the wave bottoms in an advance, and to the line that slopes down across the wave tops in a decline. And we noted that the opposite reversal points (i.e., the wave crests in an advance and the wave troughs in a decline), were, as a rule, less clearly delimited. That is one of the reasons that our discussion up to this point has been devoted to basic trendlines. Another reason is, of course, that the technician's

Chart 22. Oracle with Trend Channel and Earnings Gap. Oracle habitually forms nice smooth trend channels often consolidated by rectangles and sideways channels. It also frequently hits air pockets, usually caused by news or earnings announcements. Frequently enough that a clever technician might hedge all or part before earnings announcements. Oracle seems sufficiently known and regular to offer a good investment vehicle, but the frequent gaps and air pockets should be programmed into the trading strategy — for example, the long-term investor might disregard them, but that would involve a different kind of vigilance — say, a long-term moving average as a warning, or an ear to the wind as to the fundamental prospects of the company, say, by checking Value Line. Also secondary and intermediate trends should not be ignored. Courtesy of AIQ, www.aiq.com.

most urgent task is to determine when a trend has run out, and, for that purpose, the basic line is all-important.

In a fair share of normal trends, however, the minor waves are sufficiently regular to be defined at their other extremes by another line. That is, the tops of the rallies composing an intermediate advance sometimes develop along a line which is approximately parallel to the basic trendline projected along their bottoms. This parallel might be called the return line because it marks the zone where reactions (return moves against the prevailing trend) originate. The area between basic trendline and return line is the trend channel.

Nicely defined trend channels appear most often in actively traded stocks of large outstanding issues and least often in the less popular and the relatively thin equities which receive only sporadic attention from investors. The value of the trend channel concept for the technical trader would hardly seem to require extended comment.

Its greatest utility, however, is not what usually appeals to the beginner when he first makes its acquaintance, namely, the determination of good profit-taking levels. Experienced technicians, rather, find it more helpful in a negative sense. Thus, once a trend channel appears to have become well established, any failure of a rally to reach the return line (top parallel of the channel in an intermediate advance) is taken as a sign of deterioration of the trend. Further, the margin by which a rally fails to reach the return line (before turning down) frequently equals the margin by which the basic trendline is penetrated by the ensuing decline before a halt or throwback in the latter occurs.

By the same token, given an established trend channel, when a reaction from the return line fails to carry prices all the way back to the basic trendline but bottoms out somewhere above it, the advance from that bottom will usually push up out of the channel on the top side (through the return line) by a margin approximately equal to the margin by which the reaction failed to reach the bottom of the channel (basic trendline).

ILLUSTRATIONS OF TREND FORMATION
AND TREND LINE DRAWING

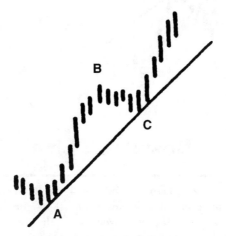

Uptrend Line

Diagram 9.   Construction of Uptrend Line — the Bullish Trendline. Even before drawing a trendline an uptrend may be distinguished by a continuing pattern of higher highs and lower lows. The trendline is then drawn through the lows of two or more reactions. Old chartists find this process so natural they may become inarticulate when asked by young chartists to explain the process and mutely point to a chart or two or hundreds. Just find two lows and lay a ruler across it. This is easy in retrospect, when the whole chart is before us. In real time it may be a different matter for the beginner. And, in fact, in real life, it is a process of recognizing a pattern formation — a rectangle, say — and marking it, and when the breakout has occurred taking the last logical down point of the rectangle, or the first reaction thereafter, to construct an experimental trendline which hangs out in the air as real trading takes place until one finds basing points on which to anchor the line. Basing points are used advisedly. In fact, the basing-points procedure discussed in the caption of Chart 27 can be used, as can other clear reactions that have clearly run their course. In real trading a constant process of drawing and redrawing takes place. For example, each time a consolidation takes place in a trend the trendline changes. The reader will see how the process has occurred in many of the charts in this book.

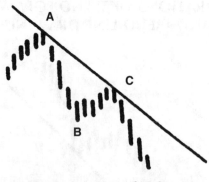

Downtrend Line

Diagram 10. Construction of Downtrend Line — the Bearish Line. The comments on construction of an uptrend line could almost be turned on their head to describe the construction of the downtrend line. The line pictured is the ideal theoretical calm drifting downtrend: lower highs, lower lows, a continuing process. The process is unmistakable though, and one should begin to see prices cross previously drawn uptrend lines and lines drawn from support and resistance from previous time in the chart. As with the uptrend line, basing points may be established and used, and often prices will fall away from the line entirely. Alternatively, rallies in the bear trend may be used to construct a line, always keeping in mind that one wants clear points on the chart and patience must be exercised in allowing the chart to develop — like a photograph coming clear in developing fluid.

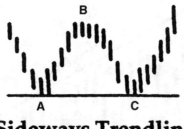

Sideways Trendline

Diagram 11.   Construction of Sideways Trendlines. A Mulish Trend? One could easily confound random walkers by semantical tricks — that is, by saying that prices are always in one kind of trend or the other — up, down, or sideways, which is, in fact, true. Sideways trendline construction is that time when prices stubbornly, like a mule, refuse to go up or down but drift horizontal or near horizontal, offering the analyst two or more points to draw a line near level across the chart. This may be described, of course, as a rectangle, or in Dow Theory as a "line." The nature of these sideways trends depends to a certain extent on the broader market mood. For example, in the volatile irrationally exuberant markets of the *fin de siecle*, it was common to see spikes up and down out of the otherwise easily definable sideways pattern. In these cases it is necessary to draw more than one line to define the sideways trend, picking the various lows at various levels. The longer these sideways trends persist, the greater their import. For example, from 1965 to 1982 the Dow was in a broad swinging sideways trend, then marched from 1000 to 11700 from 1982 to 2000. See Charts 4 and 51.

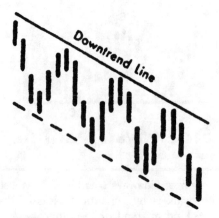

Downtrend Channel

Diagram 12. Formation of Downtrend Channel. The downtrend channel pictured here is a nice orderly retreat without panic on one side or enthusiasm on the other. This kind of emotion produces an orderly, easily defined trend channel. It's a nice coherent picture of price deterioration. Obviously the technician will be short. Anyone long at this point is not an experienced technician. The experienced practitioner will be short and watching the lines defining the channel because it is unlikely that it will last forever. Failure to touch the return line — in other words, an acceleration of the trend for the aggressive trader — might be a signal to pyramid, or, more conservatively put, to position build, although whichever you call it, pyramiding is less dangerous on the short side than on the long. (Except at market tops when selling strength.) The channel is important only as long as it continues, but its mere existence allows the analyst to get the rhythm and state of the particular issue involved.

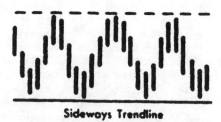

Sideways Trendline

Sideways Channel

Diagram 13. Formation of Sideways Channel. Like the up and down channels, the sideways channel represents an understandable, manageable, situation. As the downtrend pictures an orderly preponderance of sellers over buyers, and the uptrend presents an orderly preponderance of buying over selling, the sideways trend channel pictures a balance between the forces. Like all trends it should be expected to continue, and like all trends the longer it continues the less probable is its continuation. It is true that the longer it continues the farther it will go when it breaks out and finds its valid direction.

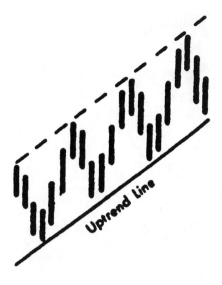

Uptrend Channel

Diagram 14.   Formation of Uptrend Channel. Many of the comments made of the down-trend channel might also be made of the uptrend channel. This uptrend channel represents the orderly advance of prices with only enough stock being offered to satisfy but not quench demand, and reasonable supplies are called forth by higher prices. There are, of course, less orderly channels, meaning broader and more difficult to confine within two lines, and when the channel becomes completely disorderly it has lost its usefulness and other interpretations must be called on. It is worth noting, in regard to this point, that when the pattern or situation does not lend itself to any understanding on the part of the technician, he should either abandon the issue in question or trade it with a high/low system or a moving average. The important matter about the trend channel, up or down, is that it gives the analyst a firm handle on what is happening at the time. It also gives him a firm handle on what can be expected to happen. First, the trend itself should continue, even if the channel becomes disorderly. If price falls short of the return line it is a yellow light, and if it then breaks the uptrend line a selling decision may soon be involved, depending on the stop methodology the trader is using. Alternatively, if price soars through the return line a different blow-off strategy may be called for, or near progressive stops.

4

OTHER IMPORTANT PATTERNS OF SHORT-TERM IMPORT: GAPS, SPIKES, REVERSALS

GAPS

A gap in the language of the chart technician represents a price range at which (at the time it occurred) no shares changed hands. This is a useful concept to keep in mind because it helps to explain some of the technical consequences of gaps.

Gaps on daily charts are produced when the lowest price at which a certain stock is traded on any one day is higher than the highest price at which it was traded on the preceding day, or when the highest price of one day is lower than the lowest price of the preceding day. When the ranges of any two such days are plotted they will not overlap or touch the same horizontal level on the chart. There will be a price gap between them. For a gap to develop on a weekly chart it is necessary that the lowest price recorded at any time in one week be higher than the highest recorded during any day of the preceding week. This can happen, of course, and does, but, for obvious reasons, not as often as daily gaps. Monthly chart gaps are rare in actively traded issues; their occurrence is confined almost entirely to those few instances in which a panic decline commences just before the end of a month and continues through the first part of the succeeding month.

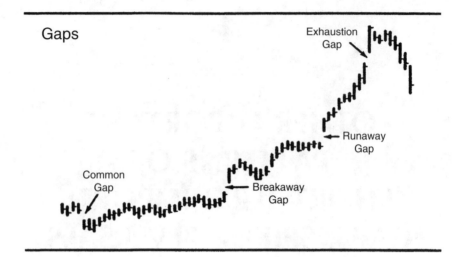

Diagram 15. Diagram Illustrating Different Kinds of Gaps. There is more than one lesson to be learned in studying gaps. The first and obvious lesson is the specific, about gaps *qua* gaps. That is, there are common gaps, breakaway gaps, runaway gaps, and exhaustion gaps. Common gaps occur within patterns or formations or trading ranges and have little if any significance. In fact, it might be said their main significance is to confirm the fact that price is confined to a congestion area. Breakaway gaps are generally pretty obvious as they occur after a congestion area and break away from its upper or lower boundary on noticeable volume. There cannot be a runaway gap without a breakaway gap, so by definition the second gap after a breakaway should be a runaway gap. It is possible that the second gap will be an exhaustion gap, and this would be explainable on analyzing the post gap action and the nature of the pattern and breakaway gap that proceeded it. Ordinarily though, a runaway gap will be the second gap and mark the power of buyers over sellers. It is also common for the runaway gap to be followed by price continuation as far as price has come from the breakout. In other words, if symmetry reigns, the breakaway will be halfway of the move. Then as the move peters out another gap *appears* which would seem to be even more buyer enthusiasm; and in fact it may be yet another runaway gap. (This is not unusual in commodities.) If this subsequent gap is an exhaustion gap, it will soon be covered and price will lose its steam. The exhaustion gap may be prelude to a blowoff, in which case it will appear to be another runaway gap, but a short time will reveal the truth.

The second lesson to be learned from the study of gaps is a general lesson which is not just about gaps but about all market phenomena. That lesson is about context and situation. In other words, the importance and significance of any pattern, formation, or market action lies not in itself alone. It must be interpreted in context. Context means the general condition of the market, the broad trend, the secondary trend, and market volatility. In addition, the same factors must be evaluated for the specific issue.

Thus a gap occurring within the obvious context of a rectangle is a common gap, but a gap leaping out of the rectangle on volume is a breakaway. Similarly, a key reversal day occurring after a 5% advance in conditions of average volatility will not have the same importance as a key reversal day occurring after a 100% advance, surging volatility, and irrational exuberance. The pattern and the gestalt. Not a knee-jerk reaction. That is what is important.

The Common or Area Gap

This type of gap gets its name from its tendency to occur within a trading area or price congestion pattern. All the congestion formations we have studied in the preceding chapters — both reversal and consolidation types — are attended by a diminution in trading turnover. The more strictly defined sorts — the triangles and rectangles — show this characteristic most conspicuously. Moreover, activity in these patterns tends to be concentrated at or near the top and bottom edges, their support and resistance lines, while the area in between is a sort of "no-man's land." It is easy to see, therefore, why gaps develop frequently within such areas. The charts show many good examples of pattern gaps.

Such pattern gaps are usually closed within a few days, and, for obvious reasons, before the congestion formation in which they have appeared is completed and prices break away from it. But not always. Sometimes a gap develops in the last traverse of prices across the pattern area just before a breakout, and in such cases it is not likely to be closed for a long time, nor is there any reason why it should be.

The forecasting significance of common or pattern gaps is practically nil. They have some use to the technician simply because they help him recognize an area pattern — that is, their appearance implies that a congestion formation is in process of construction. If, for example, a stock moves up from 10 to 20, drops back to 17, and then returns to 20 making a gap in the course of that rally, it is a fair assumption that further pattern development will take place between approximately 17 and 20. This is a convenient thing to know and may, on occasion, be turned to profit in short-term trading.

Pattern gaps are more apt to develop in consolidation than in reversal formations. Thus, the appearance of many gaps within an evolving rectangle or symmetrical triangle reinforces the normal expectation that the pattern in question will turn out to be a consolidation rather than a reversal area.

Breakaway Gaps

The breakaway type of gap also appears in connection with a price congestion formation, but it develops at the completion of the formation in the move that breaks prices away. Any breakout through a horizontal pattern boundary, such as the top of an ascending triangle, is likely to be attended by a gap. In fact, it is safe to say that most of them are attended by a gap. And, if we consider what goes on in the market to create a flat-topped price formation, it is easy to see why breakaway gaps should be expected. An ascending triangle, for example, is produced by persistent demand for a stock meeting a large supply of it for sale at a fixed price. Suppose that supply is being distributed at 40. Other holders of the stock who may have intended originally to liquidate at 40½ or 41 see quotations come up to 40 time after time, stop there, and turn back. They tend, in consequence, either to join the crowd selling at 40, or else to figure that, once through 40, prices will go much higher; they may either lower or raise their selling price. The result is a "vacuum" on the books, a dearth of offerings in the price range immediately above the pattern. Hence, when the supply at 40 in our ascending triangle example is finally all absorbed, the next buyer of the stock finds none offered at 40⅛ or 40¼, and he has to bid up a point or more to get his shares, thus creating a breakaway gap.

Continuation or Runaway Gaps

Less frequent in their appearance than either of the two forms we discussed previously, gaps of the continuation or runaway type are of far greater technical significance because they afford a rough indication of the probable extent of the move in which they occur. For that reason, they are sometimes called measuring gaps.

Both the common or pattern gap and the breakaway gap develop in association with price formations of the area or congestion type, the former within the formation and the latter as prices move out of it. The runaway gap, on the other hand, as well as the exhaustion gap, which is discussed later, is not associated with area patterns but occurs in the course of rapid, straight-line advances or declines.

When a dynamic move starts from an area of accumulation, the upward trend of prices often seems to gather "steam," to accelerate for a few days, perhaps a week or more, and then begins to lose momentum as supply increases when the extent of the advance invites more and more profit taking. Trading volume jumps to a peak on the initial breakout, tapers off somewhat in the middle of the advance, and then leaps up again to a terrific turnover as the move is finally halted. In such moves — and in rapid declines of corresponding character — a wide gap is quite likely to appear when the runaway is at its most intense, when quotations are moving most rapidly and easily with relation to the volume of transactions. That period comes normally at just about the halfway point between the breakout that inaugurated the move and the reversal day or congestion pattern that calls an end to it.

Exhaustion Gaps

The breakout gap signals the start of a move; the runaway gap marks its rapid continuation at or near its halfway point; the exhaustion gap comes

Chart 23.   IBM, Double Top in a Relatively Complex Situation. IBM tells an interesting and instructive story in this chart, beginning with a breakaway gap, a large breakaway gap on impressive volume. A trade on the breakout day would have been completely justifiable technically. The second gap, which should be a runaway gap, is quickly covered, but until this reaction there has been no point on which to place a trendline. Subsequent reactions give other points for even tighter trendlines. If a trader were trading a multilevel (or multiunit) position, the liquidation of a unit on the gap through the trendline in July would be indicated. Another unit might be taken off with the breaking of the trendline in August. The failure of the advance in September is ominous and one might immediately begin to suspect a double top. The drop through the neckline at 117 is ample notice to abandon hope, a propitious warning in view of the plunge in October. It is interesting but not coincidental that the price drop is arrested around the support level of 94. Among the other interesting lessons here is the rectangle that makes the bottom in October and November.

at the end. The first two of these are easily distinguished as to type by their location with respect to the preceding price pattern, but the last is not always immediately distinguishable from the second.

Exhaustion gaps, like runaway gaps, are associated with rapid, extensive advances or declines. We have described the runaway type as the sort that occurs in the midst of a move, that accelerates to high velocity, then slows down again, and finally stops as increasing resistance overcomes its momentum.

Chart 24. Consolidated Edison. If we take the history from early 1965, when it reached its all-time high of 49¼, we find that like almost all of the other electric utilities, ED had declined more than 50% by 1973. And, like most other utilities, the dividends were steady, and the earnings good. But, at 18, the stock did not look healthy as you can see. And then on Tuesday, April 23, the bottom fell out completely, and, within 4 weeks, it was down to 7, later to 6. The stock was not showing strength at any point in 1974. It did not look like "a bargain" at 18. And it most certainly did not look like a bargain at any time after the great downside gap. ED is unusual only in that the breakdown was so spectacular. Actually, other stocks in the group have also looked unattractive to buy or sell. And rather than considering these as "bargains," we would be asking why, if they are so good, should they be passed over by the important institutions in Wall Street? It would take some solid evidence of assertive, eager buying to make these utilities look good. In a situation like this, it would seem best to stay out or sell short.

AAPL LAST-Weekly 12/01/2000

Created with TradeStation www.TradeStation.com

Chart 25. Apple, Brought Low by Earnings Hysteria. The infamous earnings gaps from the turn of the millennium. As the Great Clinton–Gore bull market began to top in 1999 and 2000 it became obvious that shorting stocks that had soon to report earnings was a profitable tactic. As almost all stocks were overbought and selling at very high price earnings ratios there was little risk in a company's reporting surprising earnings. On the other hand, the least disappointment in earnings figures resulted in breathtaking punishment by traders. Earnings gaps of 6% — even up to 43% — occurred. Easy money for the alert trader.

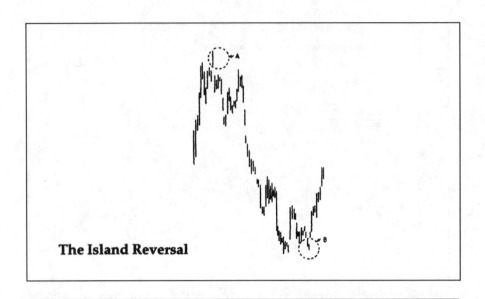

The Island Reversal

Diagram 16. Diagram of Island Reversal. The island reversal has been chosen here because its meaning is so clear and obvious. Even the novice should have no difficulty reading the message. It is like an exclamation mark at the end of a long sentence. Note that it should be at the end of a long sentence. Just as we discussed in the case of gaps, the context must be evaluated.

And what is the other important matter about the island reversal, the general matter which it has in common with all market phenomena? That, like all market phenomena, you do not know definitively the nature of the pattern until it is complete. As in all technical analysis, patience is required to allow the market to complete the message. That is why, besides intelligence, patience is the most important attribute of a trader.

The Island Reversal

The island pattern is not common and it is not, in itself, of major significance, in the sense of denoting a long-term top or bottom, but it does, as a rule, send prices back for a complete retracement of the minor move that preceded it.

An island reversal might be described as a compact trading range separated from the move that led to it (and which was usually fast) by an exhaustion gap, and from the move in the opposite direction that follows it (and which is also equally fast, as a rule) by a breakaway gap. The trading range may consist of only a single day, in which event it normally develops as a one-day reversal, or it may be made up of several days to a week or so of minor fluctuations within a compact price zone. It is characterized, as might be expected, by relatively high volume. The gaps at either end occur at approximately the same price level (they should overlap to some extent) so that the whole area stands out as an island on the chart, isolated by the gaps from the rest of the price path.

We have said that an island does not of itself appear as a major reversal formation, but islands frequently develop within the larger patterns at turning points of primary or important intermediate consequence, as, for example, in the head of a dynamic head-and-shoulders top. By the same token, they appear occasionally at the extremes of the minor swings that compose a triangle or a rectangle (in which event, of course, the gaps that set them off are really better classified as common or pattern gaps).

The reasons islands can and do develop — in other words, why gaps can and do repeat at the same price level — become more apparent when we think back on the general subject of support and resistance (see Chapter 2). Suffice it to repeat, at this point, that prices can move most rapidly and easily, either up or down, through a range where little or no stock changed hands in the past, in other words, where previous owners have no "vested interest."

Sometimes, the second gap — the breakaway that completes the island — is closed a few days later by a quick pullback or reaction. More often it is not. Rarely, the first gap — the exhaustion gap that starts the island — is covered in a few days before the second gap appears, in which event the island congestion takes on a sort of V-shape (if it is a top), and there is no clear "open water" across the chart horizontally between the island and the trends preceding and following it. In any of these variations, however, the interpretation remains the same: The preceding minor move should be practically retraced.

OTHER DAILY PATTERNS OF POTENTIAL SIGNIFICANCE: SPIKES, RUNAWAY DAYS, REVERSAL DAYS, KEY REVERSAL DAYS

Daily patterns obviously have less importance than, say, a long-term head-and-shoulders or a massive reversal formation. But they often occur at critical junctures and sometimes give trading signals worth paying attention to. They also appear in circumstances in which they have little importance. Being able to tell the difference comes from experience and study. And there is always the chance to be wrong when taking action based on their appearance.

Spikes

A spike is a day whose bar on the chart protrudes markedly above the previous and succeeding days. Clearly at the time it occurs the trader does not know whether it is a runaway day (see below) or a spike. The Errol Flynn (or Indiana Jones) type trader though, if possessed of exquisite timing and judgment and luck, might catch a market top by correctly identifying the day as a spike at the moment, thus selling short at the top. The gold markets of the 1980s ended with just such a spike. And one of my associates sold it short at $1000 an ounce: a nice trade. When making this trade the trader must be prepared to experience subsequent run days (runaway days) against his position.

Reversal Days

Sometimes a spike is also a reversal day — that is, a day on which the price opens strong, takes off like a rocket, pierces new highs, and then reverses and closes on the low. If long, this is not a pleasant sign and is worth close watching — and, perhaps, depending on the status of the market, may justify a hasty exit.

Runaway, or Run Days

A day on which the price opens strong and pushes up (or down) all day long and ends on strength, transversing a range notably greater than average days is a run day or runaway day. Such days tend to occur in the latter stages of bull markets, perhaps with a gap involved. Of a lesser magnitude they may occur on breakouts (*see Chart 26*).

Chart 26. Lucent, Illustrating Key Reversal Days. As the great Clinton–Gore bull market expired, many high-flying stocks developed long rectangles and congested trading patterns, offering easy low-risk opportunities for short scalps on key reversal day patterns. Some stocks are better for this than others, and study of the stock itself is advised before this or any other trading strategy like this is implemented.

Key Reversal Days

At the turn of the millennium, key reversal days appeared frequently in the charts of tech issues offering good trading opportunities. A key reversal day occurs when today's high is higher than yesterday's, and today's close is lower than yesterday's.

For the agile trader these patterns can afford good trading signals if evaluated properly. For the longer-term investor they can be yellow caution lights, blinking red lights, or even stop signs.

5

WHEN TO BUY, WHEN TO SELL: STOPS, HAIR-TRIGGER STOPS, PROGRESSIVE STOPS

STOPS

Stop orders, or as everyone refers to them, stops, are the instructions given to the broker or the market or the computer to buy or sell a security depending on specific criteria. For example, "Sell my 100 shares of IBM if the market price declines to 99." Or, "Buy 100 shares of IBM if the price rises to 101." Stops may be used as indicated for buying and selling. Here in this discussion we are concerned only with the use of stops for protective purposes, that is, to stop a loss from running, or to protect an accumulated profit.

First, no stop system is perfect. Regardless of the way stops are calculated, and there are myriad ways, losses will occur, profits will not be efficiently seized, money will be left on the table. It is unfortunately an imperfect world. *But* almost any stop system is better than indecision, confusion, and doubt. John Magee developed a number of stop systems, all of them good. Their use often depends on the particular market situation and can be relatively complex (consult *Technical Analysis of Stock Trends*, 8th ed.), but here we cover the basics.

Two situations exist in which stops should be calculated and used: entry and profit protection.

INITIAL STOP LOSS CALCULATION

When we make an initiating trade, buying or shorting a stock, we must, even before completing the transaction, compute a stop to limit the loss if the market moves against our position. Such a move is almost guaranteed to occur in trend trading. The way we deal with counter moves is to plan the trade so as to limit the loss up front. There are two ways to set the initial stop — using a money management rule or finding a technically analyzed point.

In the first case the trader would determine the percentage risk to be taken from the entry price and set the stop that distance below the entry (e.g., entry price 100; percentage risk 8%; stop price 92). Or, on the same trade the analyst might have found a support level at 95 — the bottom of a rectangle or a triangle support line — and set his stop there. Or, he might find the support level and add a fudge factor — 2% or 3% to the support level. Say, 95 plus 2 or 93. In either case the sum at risk is called (by this author) the *Operational Risk*.

It is entirely possible that the market will take out this stop. It is also entirely possible that IBM will decline to 20, making the stop at 93 look like an act of genius. For the wisdom of this kind of policy see the "Best and Brightest Case" (Appendix A, page 149).

PROTECTING AN ACCUMULATING PROFIT WITH ADVANCING STOPS

A happier situation exists when our trade has worked out well and over time has accumulated paper profits. Paper profits are real profits. They are not illusory. It is as improvident to allow paper profits to dissolve as it is to allow a loss to run for not having a stop entered (*see Case 21, Appendix A, pg. 190*). Experiences of this kind are warning signals to an investor, warning signals which may be a notice that further education is necessary, or that an investment psychiatrist should be consulted. (Start by reading *Winning the Mental Game on Wall Street* by John Magee.)

THE ANALYZED STOP, COMPUTED FROM THE CHART

As our stock advances it performs all the gyrations described in this book. It proceeds in a straight line up. Profit taking occurs and it falls back, perhaps as much as 50% of its run, or it drifts sideways into a rectangle, or a triangle as buyers and sellers contest the ground. It breaks out, perhaps in a gap, runs and returns to the breakout line, then battles for a few points. In short it is EveryMan's EveryStock. The reader of this book should have by now some idea of how to deal with these situations. He is looking for support and resistance levels, for trading and congestion zones, for trendlines and trend channels. He is learning to recognize changes of trend, signs of strength, and signs of weakness. He is also defining his personal trading style and philosophy.

Perhaps he operates on the basis of support/resistance levels, or only on trendlines. I have known successful traders who used both, or only one. Nevertheless, he finds the line significant to him, and uses it, or it plus a filter such as 2% or 3%. So when price breaks the chosen line by 2% it finds his stop and he takes the rest of the money to the bank. Naturally, he gave some of it back. If he did not give some back he is not letting his profits run until a definite change of trend is proven to have occurred. I call this the Bridge Rule, after a comment by Goren that if a declarer didn't get set on at least 20% of his contracts he was underbidding.

PROGRESSIVE STOPS, OR THE 3-DAYS-AWAY PROCEDURE

Another way of advancing stops is from a procedure developed by Magee called awkwardly the *3-days-away procedure*, or, sometimes, the *basing-points procedure*.

Using this procedure the analyst determines basing points as follows:

1. He observes low price points on reactions.
2. He watches the market until 3 days of price activity outside the range of the low day have occurred.
3. This price low is then marked as the basing point.
4. The stop is then computed based on this point. The stop might be the point itself, or a close below it, or the point plus a filter which might range from 2% to 8%.

This is a summary of the process. It is actually more complex and more clever than this brief description would imply, but the procedure described here is certainly sufficient for the purposes of the general investor and considerably more sophisticated than any process used by the average unenlightened investor.

Let me emphasize that this brief discussion only scratches the surface of the subject of stop setting — *and* it is sufficient for the general long-term investor. Chapter 8, on moving averages, discusses other methods.

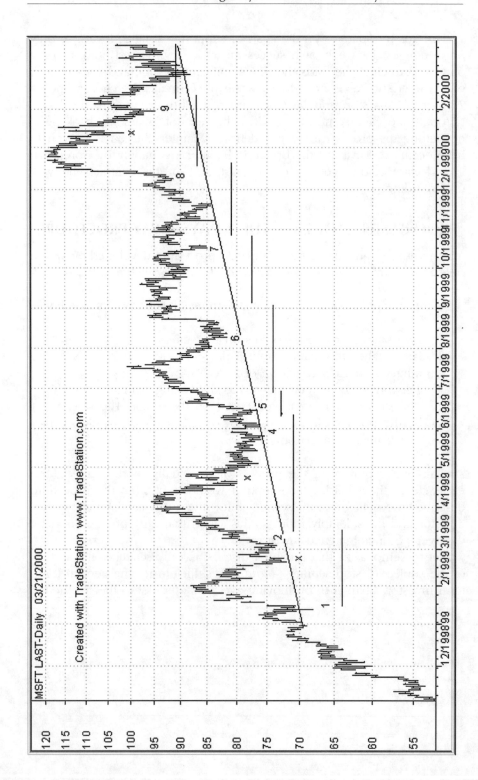

Chart 27. Microsoft, Illustrating Stop-Setting with 3-Days-Away-Procedure. This is, perhaps, the most important chart in this book. Illustrated is a stop-setting procedure Magee called progressive stops using basing points. In using this procedure the trader finds the low of a reaction against the trend. To become a basing point the price must spend a minimum of 3 days above the range of the basing-point day. Once that has occurred the stop is set at the basing point less the filter. The filter is a percentage figure which may vary according to the volatility of the stock. As a rough rule of thumb the filter would range for most stops from 5% to 8%; 5% has been used on this chart of Microsoft. (Please note that prices are rough-cut on this chart.) Thus, at 1 where the low is 68 the stop is set at 64.60. When the low at 2 occurs and prices move 3 days out of range above, the stop is raised to 70.12, 5% below 73.81. x now occurs between 3 and 4, appearing to be a potential basing point. However the price comes back before it has closed 3 days out of range, and higher. This makes 4 the next basing point which meets our criteria, and at 75 the stop is raised to 71.25. 5 is the next basing point at 76.625 with a stop at 72.79. No sufficient reaction occurs between 5 and 6 (generally speaking we want to see a reaction that brings price back about half way or more). The top between 5 and 6 definitely heightens attention, looking like a spike. Following the procedure of hair-trigger or near progressive stops, some traders might set a stop ⅛ under the spike day and be taken out shortly. The longer-term trader would have found a new basing point at 6 (81.625 and 77.54). A rectangle develops with 7 as one of its points and also as a basing point (85.063 and 80.80). Between 7 and 8, price comes back as might well be expected but, because of the filter of 5%, leaves the position intact. The reaction cannot be taken as a basing point because that would cause a lowering of the stop which is against the rules. The reaction at 8, though small, offers another point, perhaps more judgmental, moving the stop to 86.87 in relation to the point at 91.438. Between 8 and 9 the x indicates a point which does not see 3 days of action away from the price on the upside, but 9 does (94.875 and 90.13). Then in an interesting development the trade is terminated in late February by the basing point stop, and, coincidentally(?) the 14-month-long trendline is broken. Note the horizontal resistance/support line at 96 which is also penetrated at the same time. This is, of course, the top of the Microsoft bull market, and the breakout in December 1999 is of course a cruel joke — sometimes known as a bull trap. The technical analyst has numerous tools to exercise here — the trendline, the basing points, the runaway days (which might be answered with the hair-trigger stop as discussed for the spike between 5 and 6), the round over after the runaway days and the return to the base of the runaway days (which might be taken as a throwback, but certainly not after the relative high after 9), and the failure of the support line at 96. In the markets of the millennium, these runaway days occurred many times and the result was almost always dismaying.

III

MAGEE'S METHODOLOGY: RISK MANAGEMENT, PORTFOLIO MANAGEMENT, AND RHYTHMIC TRADING. PRAGMATIC PORTFOLIO THEORY FROM PROFESSOR BASSETTI.

The Magee method is briefly summarized, and Bassetti develops and articulates Magee's ideas of rhythmic investing, portfolio management, and risk management and control.

To manage and control the risks associated with stock trading, investors must observe a variety of common sense procedures. A portfolio should be diversified and balanced. It should attune itself to the nature of the market — that is, it should do as the market does: trade some longs and trade some shorts. The Magee Evaluative Index (MEI) offers a way to allocate assets according to the character of the market. Observing the principles of this Index (which is a stratification of the market into longs' shorts and neutrals) leads to rhythmic trading. Rhythmic trading is the liquidation of positions as the markets move, mature, and change and the initiation of new positions in the direction indicated by the MEI. Thus as a bull market tops out, longs would be closed and shorts would be put on in a natural rhythmic process.

Pragmatic Portfolio Theory offers investors a coherent simple way to assess and control the risk of their trades and portfolio.

6

THE MAGEE METHOD

John Magee Inc.'s method of portfolio strategy for technical investing is diversification by industry, geographic diversification, diversification by type of investment, and a systematic strategy for minimizing losses and maximizing gains known as the trailing (*or progressive*) stop method of trend following. For purposes of this discussion, however, we are only referring to the common stock position of one's portfolio. Protective stops are used for both long and short positions. After a purchase has been made, a price is selected below which the stock will be sold at the market. This price is defined as the protective limit. It fixes (with rare exceptions) in advance how much we are willing to lose on a position. As a position moves higher, the limit is advanced. As long as a trend "goes our way," we hold the stock and advance the limit. As soon as the trend is broken, and the protective limit violated, we sell at the market.

PORTFOLIO STRATEGIES: LIQUIDITY, INDUSTRY SELECTION, AND NUMBER OF POSITIONS

How many stock positions should an investor own at one time? Which stocks should be included once the "ideal" number of positions has been determined? The answers to these seemingly straightforward questions are, in fact, quite complex because portfolio strategy depends in part on the needs and characteristics of each individual investor. The range of possible outcomes is extremely wide. Perhaps the most common mistake we have observed is the investor is buying small positions in so many stocks that he has trouble following them all (*see Case 9, Appendix A*). Moreover, each position tends to be such a small part of the whole that even a good job of managing a holding has little impact on the investor's total holdings.

The opposite extreme, that of "putting all one's eggs in one basket and then watching the basket closely," carries the obvious risk that a single "bad" investment could wipe out a significant portion of one's assets.

Our experience suggests that portfolio diversification and managerial efficiency combine usefully when the number of positions varies from 2 to 10 and funds available for investment vary from $10,000 to $200,000. For example, if an investor has $10,000 to invest initially, we would recommend the selection of two positions of $5000 and $5000 each. A $100,000 investor might begin with 6 or 7 positions of $15,000 each. While at $200,000, approximately 10 positions averaging $20,000 each would be appropriate. The benefits of diversification decline sharply as the number of positions held rises above 10; thus, for even a $1 million account, we would recommend holding no more than 10 to 12 positions. *(As the reader will see, the Editor feels these ideas were later refined by Magee more in the directions recommended in the next chapter. In addition it is my feeling that a $10,000 portfolio is probably better off in ishares than in individual stocks; see Case 24, Appendix A.)*

Additional diversification criteria that we have found useful include industry and liquidity. For a theoretical $120,000 portfolio of eight $15,000 positions, we certainly would not want all eight positions to be in steel, or oil, or electronics, or any other single industry. Thus, we suggest a policy of individual stock selection that provides industry diversification. For our theoretical $120,000 portfolio, a "concentration limitation" of two holdings in any one industry (25% of total portfolio) is desirable, with one position per industry being ideal.

To the extent that one's stock positions become sizable (1000 shares and up of a stock), we add "liquidity." As a stock position totals 100 shares or even a few hundred shares of a nationally listed company, a high degree of liquidity can be assumed. But when it is time to head for the exits with larger positions, one's ability to sell and move quickly may be sharply reduced in many of the "thinner," less actively traded stocks that may be found on the exchanges. Our rule is that no more than half the issues in any individual industry should be illiquid.

7

FURTHER DEVELOPMENTS TO THE MAGEE METHOD: PORTFOLIO MANAGEMENT, RISK CONTROL, INCLUDING RHYTHMIC TRADING AND PRAGMATIC PORTFOLIO THEORY

THE ELEMENTS OF THE MAGEE METHOD

The Magee method is a complete and well-rounded expression of a philosophy and methodology regarding long-term success in the markets. This method might be described as midterm technical trend following, regulated by prudent diversification and disciplined risk control (including hedged portfolios) managed with unemotional realistic patience. This long sentence demands an entire book for its complete explication. The book in fact exists, and is, of course, *Technical Analysis of Stock Trends*, now in its eighth edition, with more than 1 million copies in print. Repeating the entire book here would be awkward, but we can attempt a summarization of Magee's method.

The essence of the Magee method is moderation. The foundations of the method may be described as follows: (1) technical analysis, (2) portfolio construction, (3) risk measurement and control, and (4) personal psychological management.

Technical Analysis

By technical analysis Magee meant the bar charting and dispassionate analysis of objective data from the markets — primarily price and volume. Charting the markets and acting on hard data alone not only mean the choice of objective data as the input to analalysis. They also mean the deliberate shunning of fundamental analysis, that is, the study of earnings, cash flow, sales figures, and on and on — that is all the data that can be manipulated and misrepresented or cooked by creative accountants. *The Wall Street Journal* does not misreport the data for trading on the New York Stock Exchange. Like the sports scores, that is not permitted in our society. But earnings reports are only as good as the integrity of the people who make them. Technical analysis also means ignoring the din of touts, brokerage house recommendations, tips from barbers and taxi drivers, and, worse, television talking heads (except for the coauthor).

This choice of an analytical method is complemented by the observation that the most efficient trading horizon or term is the mid- to long-term trend. Mid- to long-term trends, in general, last at the extreme several years but might be only months in duration, as opposed to a secular trend which might last many years — as in the case of the great bull market of the late 20th century which began in 1982 and lasted until 2000. Trading on the Dow Theory certainly was rewarding over the last century. The mid-term analyst should have done even better, not being constrained by the long periods necessary to generate signals.

Thus, in detail, Magee gathers data from the market that is uncontested — price and volume rather than hypothetical earnings. He presents these data in bar charts. From long experience and investigation he analyzes the chart and identifies situations in which the probabilities are in his favor. For example, he finds a trading range defined as a rectangle, and when price breaks out of the rectangle he commits a portion of his capital to it. At the same time, he sets a stop beneath his trade in case his experiment is unprofitable. If the market moves in his favor he systematically raises his stops to protect his profits. He pursues this policy until the trend proves to have definitively changed.

Portfolio Construction and Management

No one thinks of Magee particularly as a portfolio theoretician, and compared to present-day practitioners he might appear (appear only) a little primitive. Modern-day theorists will not have examined his work on *sensitivity* and *composite leverage*, which precede the academics' creation of modern portfolio theory. Modern-day portfolio theorists will bend themselves into pretzels computing correlations, constructing variance-co-variance matrices, investigating volatilities, and calculating portfolio Monte Carlo simulations. I think the general investor will probably find Modern Portfolio Theory a little sticky and prefer Pragmatic Portfolio Theory, as briefly summarized below.

In actuality there is much to be said for Magee's latter practice and philosophy, which might be described as *rhythmic and natural, hedged and simple*, and which I have further articulated and called Pragmatic Portfolio Theory. Pragmatic Portfolio Theory is comprehensively described in *Technical Analysis of Stock Trends* (8th ed.).

Rhythmic and Natural

I call Magee's trading approach rhythmic and natural. Natural, because it observes what the market says without intervening algorithms and takes action based on an interpretation of market activity. Rhythmic, because, for example, in a bull market turning to bear, the trader has been following the market with long positions which are liquidated as the market turns. Observing the measurements of the MEI (as explained later and in Case 24, Appendix A), as well as trading opportunities, the trader begins to turn his portfolio to the short side, putting on his new trades as shorts.

Hedged

As refers to hedged, Magee thought that a portfolio should be biased in the direction of the general market, and the percentage it should be biased in the direction of the broad market was determined by the analysis of the market, the MEI. The MEI is constructed by analyzing the market or market segment and classifying it into strong, weak, and neutral layers. This creates a kind of oscillator with which one may find broad market tops and bottoms. And one may also use it to allocate the portfolio to longs and shorts. If the MEI is 60% bull, then the portfolio is 60% long or thereabouts (thereabouts — is close enough; only in professional trading do teenies really matter). The rest of the portfolio is allocated to shorts and sidelines.

Simple

Magee thought, in general, leaving aside considerations of extremely large and extremely small capital, that 8 to 10 issues were sufficient diversification. His mind may have been constrained on this number because of the difficulty and distraction of managing larger more complex portfolios by manual means, but the point is at least sustainable. And, in view of comments I make later concerning present-day portfolio construction, this number is moot. We must also remember that during the mature part of his career, Magee did not have the incredible array of investment instruments available to the modern trader.

Risk Measurement and Control

Magee practiced what I call *Operational Risk Control*, never entering a position without a technically analyzed stop. If there is an essence to his philosophy and method beyond that expressed by the term "technical analysis" it is risk control. Starting with diversification, buttressed by trend following, adding probable behavior, concluding with stop calculation, Magee's method is a wholly articulated and an integral system for managing risk. It is, in fact, better than that practiced by the majority of professional portfolio managers who seem to be incapable of recognizing the escalating risk of being long a stock in a downtrend (*see Case 1, Appendix A*).

A firm understanding of these concepts is necessary because the management of risk is the one indispensable element necessary to investment success (aside from dumb luck). One of the most amusing and mysterious facts of the universe is that the best trader I know personally for risk management also is possessed of more dumb luck than any other trader I know of. Perhaps it is the Jack Nicklaus phenomenon. Jack said, "The harder I work the luckier I get."

Trend Following

The trend follower diminishes his risk by intending to take the middle third of a trend. He does not enter his position until the market has in all probability signaled its intentions. He does not exit his position until the market signals that it has reversed its direction. Bottom fishers and top pickers clearly and obviously run the greatest risks. They also, incidentally, in the short run reap the greatest profits.

Trend traders are willing to let them have those greater profits, preferring to take the least risky part of a trend — the middle third.

Diversification

If all a trader's capital is concentrated in one issue, the destruction of that issue lets him experience that most painful of trading experiences: gambler's ruin — that is, being wiped out, and not being able to play anymore, which is more distressing than losing all one's money. Magee thought

8 to 10 issues were good diversification. I think this is sufficient, and, or but, I also think that the ballast of a portfolio should be in the important averages — the Dow and the Standard & Poor's primarily, with the speculative portion in the NASDAQ. This is easily accomplished by investing in ishares, the SPY, DIA, and QQQ as traded at the AMEX.

Profit Goals and Trade Management

Attempting to make, say, spectacular profits, exposes one to spectacular risks. As Magee points out in Chapter 11, investors can take a lot of hits of their capital of 3% to 8%, but a few hits of 40% or 50% will send them back to the pinochle table. In a word, when an investor puts his trades on, he calibrates them so that his risk represents a tolerable amount of his capital.

A HINT TO THE WISE

I think it was Malraux who said, "Smart men learn from their mistakes. Wise men learn from the mistakes of others." Even in a primer the reader should learn that he must calaibrate the size loss he must plan to take on his total capital when he puts on a trade, so that instead of putting on 1000 shares of Microsoft, which represents 75% of his capital to risk, he puts on 100 shares with a planned loss of 5% of his capital, if that occurs. And, according to the MEI, it does not require a Nobel Laureate to stratify a portfolio into some longs and some shorts, or to hedge when the market is screaming "overbought!" In fact, judging from Long-Term Capital Management, one might be better off without a Nobel Laureate. By computing and aggregating operational risk for the entire portfolio the investor may see at any point in time what his risk is — a risk which will be diminished if it is somewhat hedged. If any portion of the operational risk is out of balance with the rest of the portfolio it may be recognized and sold down. Pragmatic Portfolio Theory is just what it says, practical as an old MIT engineer with only a slide rule for a sidekick.

IV

OTHER TECHNICAL ANALYSIS TOOLS: NUMBER-DRIVEN TECHNIQUES, CANDLESTICKS, AND POINT-AND-FIGURE CHARTING — ALGORITHMIC TRADING

Charting is the original form of technical analysis, the basic discipline. With the development of the computer and the Internet, other forms of technical analysis have proliferated — number-driven (or statistical) analysis, an ancient Japanese form, candlesticks, and point-and-figure analysis.

A Chacun son gout, as Andre Malraux is said to have remarked. Each to his own. Although charting is the original form of technical analysis, other forms have flourished over the last half century, especially with the advent of the computer. The computer has allowed analysts to construct and test more and more complex algorithms and to use these objective systems in the markets. Many of these number-driven methods have produced astounding profits. Some have also, after having produced astounding profits, shredded their capital: a prescient warning that nothing lasts forever, and that the market learns about successful systems and works to defeat them.

Nonetheless, number-driven tools fit the style and character of many analysts and serve them well. The neophyte would do well to know something about them. As an example, nothing more vividly illustrates a sideways market than a moving average line wandering through it.

In addition to statistical systems, two "natural" methods deserve some attention — candlesticks and point-and-figure charting (P&F). (P&F is not purely natural but close enough for government work.) Both are graphic ways of looking at the markets and may be the tool of choice for some traders. I have seen traders have success with these methods, in some cases quite notable success. These natural and "unnatural" methods are explored exhaustively in *Technical Analysis: Natural and Unnatural Methods,* Bassetti and Bassetti. (*See Appendix C.*)

8

OTHER IMPORTANT TECHNICAL ANALYSIS METHODS

A BEWILDERING ARRAY OF TOOLS AND INDICATORS

The newcomer to technical analysis will quickly be confronted with a bewildering array of tools, gadgets, and widgets. There are probably 30 or 40 such tools with some popularity, and new ones are being developed daily. These tools are well implemented in the commercially available software packages (e.g., Metastock, AIQ and TradeStation, and Wall Street Investor, which is for the Macintosh). Metastock has included in its standard tool chest six categories of technical indicators, among them indicators for trends, volatility, momentum, cycles, market strength, and support/resistance. Within these categories they include upwards of 100 separate entries. AIQ has in the neighborhood of 49. Omega TradeStation has similar numbers of studies and indicators. I cite these numbers only to indicate to the newcomer some degree of the potential richness and complexity of the field. The software packages mentioned should not be compared on this basis. Any one of them represents a challenge for the beginner. In fact, an excellent way to achieve an in-depth education in the area of number-driven systems would be to paper trade the technical indicators in any of these packages. Money trading them would be an expensive way to get an education. One should not run before walking, or walk before crawling — unless, of course, bungee jumping is one's favorite sport.

I habitually get a laugh from my technical analysis seminars by asking the rhetorical question, Why are there so many number-driven techniques? The answer, of course, is because none of them work all the time, and some work only for their inventors, or only worked very well at some given point in the past. I should not be so irreverent. Number-driven systems have often scored astounding successes. And, for those who cannot relate to graphic chart analysis, number-driven methods may be the only way to trade technically. It is also true that numbers do not change their complexion according to the amount of hope and fear inspired by the markets at any given moment.

And, also, it is my casual observation that many more traders use number-driven systems than use chart analysis — or use some combination. The reason usually given for this is that number-driven signals do not admit of misinterpretation due to terror or greed. This is a powerful factor in their favor.

These tools are here given the name "number driven (or statistical)" because they use results derived from market action to arrive at their conclusions — namely, price and volume data. Of course, all technical analysis uses these basic data, but chart-based analysis uses it in a qualitative way, whereas number-driven analysis uses it as determinative.

I make no attempt here to explore every tool in detail — I am not even persuaded that every tool is worth it. But I do attempt to give the reader a brief outline of what are, in my opinion, the most interesting.

PHILOSOPHER'S STONE FOUND

Just as chart interpretation varies from analyst to analyst, different users reach different conclusions from many of the statistical tools. It is my suspicion that when these techniques are successful, more is involved than the objective technique. In other words, the inventor (or adroit user) is unconsciously employing some unrecognized experience and judgment behind the use of the tool. How otherwise to explain the success of Larry Williams (inventor of %R, which is defined later)? On at least two occasions (that I know of) Williams has taken spectacular profits out of the markets. If %R is so good why hasn't Williams taken spectacular profits year after year? (Maybe he has. Maybe I just don't know about it.) In fact, the coincidence of market, trader, and tool creates the illusion of the philosopher's stone — found at last.

Sadly, no stone — even those not left unturned. With these words of cynicism, we will briefly examine the box of statistical tools as purely an introduction so that the novice is aware of the richness and complexity of the discipline.

WHAT DO THESE TOOLS ATTEMPT TO DO?

I habitually divide these tools into three categories: trading tools, trending tools, and volume analysis. Remember that trend systems buy strength and sell weakness, and trading systems sell strength and buy weakness. Volume analysis attempts to quantify the assessment that the chart analyst makes of the importance of volume. Although some traders employ exclusively one or the other trading or trending tool, there is no inherent conflict in using trading tools within a trend-following system in attempting to determine when to take profits or hedge. In fact, for all but the longest-term investors I believe in a diversity of tactics. The markets after all are infinite in their diversity. Why shouldn't tactics adjust continuously to them, depending, of course, on the time frame of the investor?

In fact, let me emphasize, the adjustment of technique to the market rhythm may be the most important factor in trading success. This adjustment occurs naturally for the chart-based trader.

To teach a mechanical number-driven system to make this adjustment requires more than a little mathematical and systems-building sophistication.

TRADING TOOLS THAT WILL BE DISCUSSED

"Momentum" is the term given to the direction and velocity of price movement. (Clearly the analysis hopes to measure momentum of the price and its likelihood of continuing.) Measurement and analytical tools of interest examined here are Wilder's RSI, Lane's Stochastic's, Bollinger's Bands, Rate of Change (ROC), Relative Strength, and Moving Average Convergence Divergence (MACD).

TREND IDENTIFICATION TOOLS COVERED

Primarily, I discuss moving averages here, as I believe that it is the best number-driven tool for trend identification.

VOLUME ANALYSIS CONSIDERED

Volume indicators proliferate also. On-balance volume is one of the better. Moving averages and oscillators can also be run on volume.

NATURAL METHODS

Candlestick Charting and Point and Figure charting will be illustrated and placed in perspective.

TRADING AND MOMENTUM TOOLS

The Relative Strength Index

Like diseases identified by doctors, technical tools are often linked to their creators. J. Welles Wilder invented the RSI to identify overbought and oversold conditions. The RSI attempts to measure average upmovement against average downmovement. Relative strength is charted on a vertical scale from 0 to 100. Conventionally, a reading over 70 indicates overbought and a reading under 30 oversold. These measures are computed using a weighted moving average. Other forms of this indicator sometimes use an exponential moving average. This indicator is sometimes confused with relative strength analysis which refers to the comparison of one issue with another (e.g., S&P 500 vs. the Dow). (See Chart 28 for an illustration of RSI.)

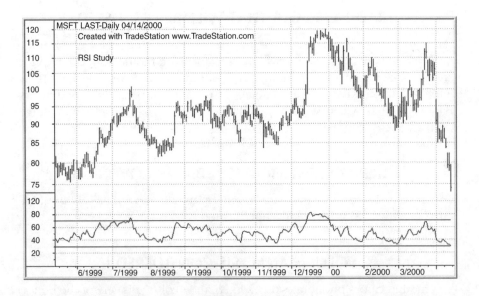

Chart 28.   Welles Wilder RSI Illustration.

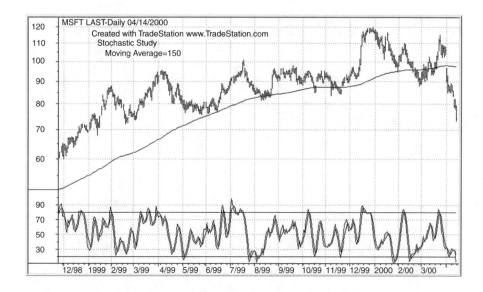

Chart 29.   George Lane Stochastic Illustration.

Stochastic Indicator

Why George Lane called the stochastic indicator "stochastic" is a mystery. The word as understood by lexicographers means "a naturally occurring random process." What Lane meant, and as the business understands it, is the relating of the closing price to the range in prices for a prior time period — usually 21 days for Lane's purposes. The idea is based on the observation or belief that in rising markets closing prices have a tendency to cluster near the top of the range, the reverse being true in downmoving markets.

The 21-day stochastic relates today's close to the price range from the previous 21-day period. The price range is the difference between the highest price and the lowest price. Expressed as a percentage, the point is plotted on a scale of 0 to 100. Above 80% is taken as overbought and below 20% is taken as oversold. Generally this tool may work well in a trading market and less well or not at all in a strongly trending market (*see Chart 29*).

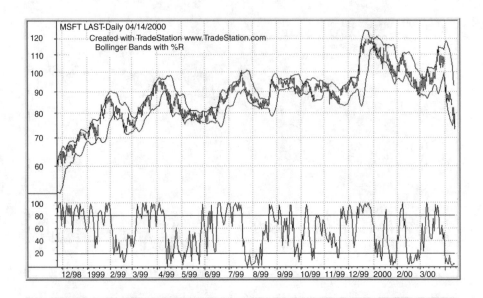

Chart 30.   Bollinger Band Illustration.

Bollinger Bands

Bollinger Bands were created by John Bollinger. Rather than an outright trading indicator, they are more a tool used in conjunction with other tools and techniques. Bollinger bands are calculated based on standard deviation from price — usually 2 standard deviations. This is charted as an envelope, above and below the price line. This means that the envelope expands and contracts about the price plot. Unusual shrinking of the envelope is usually associated with potential for price breakout (*see Chart 30*).

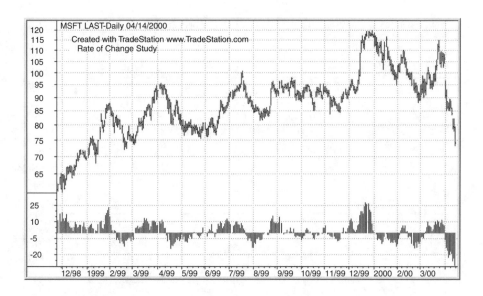

Chart 31. Rate of Change Illustration.

Rate of Change

ROC is a simple indicator, simply constructed. The present price is compared to the price *n* days ago. As an example, if the ROC were 10 days, today's price would be compared to today minus 10 days (and tomorrow's price compared with tomorrow minus 9 days). The result, plotted as a continuous series, then oscillates about an equilibrium line to give one a measure of overbought and oversold conditions. Chart 31 is a representative chart.

A ROC indicator is not a definitive or totally dependable measure of overbought and oversold conditions. A stock can go from being over-bought to being very overbought. And then to very, very overbought. And then to unbelievably overbought as those who measured it over-bought shorted it, only to see it become even more overbought. Then be caught in the boa constrictor of short squeeze. In the reverse situation, the oversold becomes very oversold, and so on.

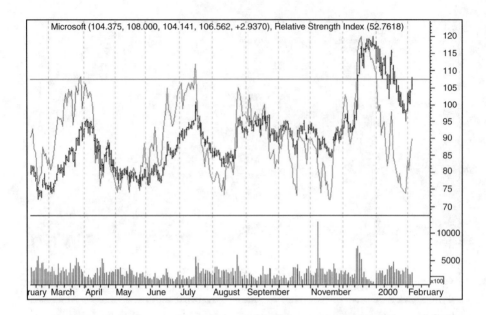

Chart 32.   Relative Strength Index Illustration.

Relative Strength Index

A potential confusion exists between the RSI and the concept of relative strength. To determine relative strength, one measurement is divided by another, but RSI is the comparison of an instrument's present status to its past behavior. As illustrated in Chart 32, it is constructed to show absolute levels of 100 and 0 with overbought conventionally set at 70 and oversold at 30. RSI exhibits the same problems of interpretation as ROC. Overbought can go to very overbought and the trader who depends on it can be left with foreshortened profits or, worse, short a rising issue. Chart created with AIQ, www.aiq.com.

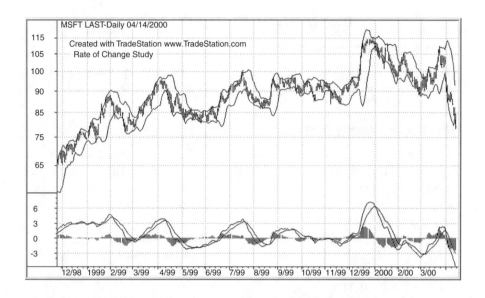

Chart 33. Moving Average Convergence/Divergence and Bollinger Bands.

Moving Average Convergence/Divergence

MACD has two elements based on exponential moving averages. The averages are computed for two different periods, commonly 12 days and 25 days. A difference is taken of these averages from which a price phase line is constructed. The second element is called a signal line, which is an exponential average of the price phase line. The common default value of the signal line is 9. Buy and sell signals are generated by the signal line crossing the price phase line (see Chart 36). Although this indicator appears gimmicky, some traders use it effectively at the end of bear trends and in the study of overbought and oversold conditions.

TREND IDENTIFICATION TOOLS

Moving Averages — The "Dynamic Trendline"

Of all the number-driven techniques, the moving average is, in my experience, the simplest and the most effective.

The Simple Moving Average

A moving average is computed by taking the number of days involved, say, 10, adding them together and dividing by length (in this case 10). The resulting point is plotted on the chart on today's date. On today plus one, the most distant day (i.e., day 1) is subtracted and the new day is added and the new sum is once again divided by 10. For example, each number representing a day and also the value of that day 1 2 3 4 5 6 7 8 9 10 = 55/10 = 5.5 is the average of the 10-day prices for today.

For the next day's price we can drop off day one and add day 11: 2 3 4 5 6 7 8 9 10 11 = 65/10 = 6.5 is the average of the 10-day prices for today plus 1.

This simple process smooths the data. As is readily seen, the difference between price 10 and price 1 is quite large. By smoothing these data we get a continuous line that is easier to see and interpret than a jagged line which may be confusing at times (*see Chart 34*).

Chart 34. The Dow, Circa 2000. A Broadening Top and Moving Average.

The Weighted Moving Average and the Exponential Moving Average

As the reader will quickly realize, a simple moving average lags price action. There are pluses and minuses to this. If the trader desires to give more weight to the most recent action he can use a weighted moving average, which will turn more quickly than the simple. To construct a weighted moving average the analyst multiplies as follows: 1st-day price by 1, 2nd-day by 2, 3rd-day by 3, and so on. Then sum and divide by the sum of the weights: 1 + 2 + 3 = 6. In the exponential variant of the moving average, the weight of the older data declines exponentially. Thus even more importance is given to recent data. This method is best examined by experimentation with a software package.

Perspective on Moving Average Methods

A moving average line has sometimes been called a "dynamic trendline," and there is some truth in this. The hand-drawn qualitative or judgmental trendline is a relatively subjective thing and depends for its validity on the experience and emotional coolness of the chartist. The moving average is totally objective. If the markets were number driven it would be a perfect tool for trading.

But, as we know by now, the markets are not number driven, and so this, like all number-driven tools, has its drawbacks as well as its strengths. Still, in my experience, moving average systems have on occasions been quite successful. And in other cases they have been a hindrance and

Chart 35. Microsoft with Two Moving Average Systems.

unprofitable. Before we examine the conditions that produce success or frustration, let us examine the context of the method and its relationship to Magee charting.

How Moving Averages Are Used

The moving average is a basic concept, and it may be used in a number of different ways. The simplest way is to buy the issue when the price crosses above the moving average and to sell the issue when the price falls below it. In a trending market this can be a powerful method. But in a sideways market it can result in numerous whipsaws depending on the length of the moving average and the rhythm of the sideways trend. A vivid illustration of this is the major market indexes at the turn of the century (*see Chart 36*).

Consequently numerous complementary methods have been developed to deal with these problems. Other tools may be used to confirm a trade. A filter may be used — that is, one does not trade until the price has moved 3% (or *x*%) over the moving average line. Or, price must stay above the line for *x* days, or must make a minimum percentage move for the trade to be taken. The more conditions put on the system the fewer trades will be taken.

This will result in fewer losses and smaller profits. It is tradeoffs such as this that drive my graduate students crazy. On the one hand this; on the other hand that, which is reminiscent of Jack Kennedy, who said that he was looking for a one-handed economist so that adviser would not be able to say, "On this hand this, ... but then on the other hand."

I examine some other aspects of moving averages further along in this chapter, but first it would be advisable to return to that old bug-a-boo: how long term is an investor? In the case of moving averages, that means how long a moving average is the investor going to use. The shorter the term, the more active the investor, until, at a certain point, he is not an investor at all but a speculator, or a trader, or even a scalper.

It is worth emphasizing here that Jorion (a superlative source on risk) in *Value at Risk* computed the following figures: mean return and probability of loss over a 1-year period, mean return: 11.1% and probability of loss: 23.6%; over an hour period, 0.0055 and 49.4%. So much for day trading.

Short, Medium, and Long-Term Moving Averages

Just as in bar charting, the trader or investor can choose a time frame that fits his character and method — short, medium, or long term. There is some consensus among technical analysts as to the parameters used for these periods which one will find embedded in the software packages, but be aware that there is nothing sacrosanct about these parameters, and furthermore the blind acceptance of these numbers makes one a member of the herd. This can sometimes be an advantage and other times a disadvantage. One would like to be more or less at the middle of the herd and able to

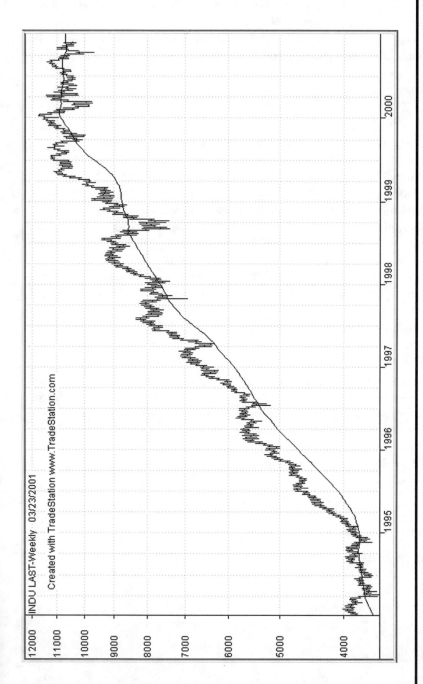

Chart 36. A 200-Day Moving Average on the Dow-Jones at the Turn of the Century. A market which slithers back and forth across a moving average is the definition of a trading range. In this case a very long-term moving average. When this occurs after the greatest bull market in history its message is clear to those who look and listen: The yellow caution light is blinking and the alarm is ringing. This behavior suspends trend trading operations, and also leads to hedging, and if so inclined, to short-term trading tactics.

stop if the herd turned out to be lemmings pouring over a cliff. And one would also like to know if it were a herd of bulls in firm control of the market.

A 10-day moving average will result in frequent trading regardless of permutations introduced. A 200-day moving average results in much slower trading. Some futures traders use 4- and 7-day moving averages, and some use these lengths as crossover signals (i.e., trading when the 4-day crosses the 7-day).

The Dow and the 150-Day Moving Average

Using a 150-day moving average on the Dow-Jones Industrials from 1897 to 1986 resulted in a 7% annual advantage over a buy-and-hold strategy. This advantage is gained using the simplest rule — buying and selling on price crossover of the average. In 1986, this strategy stopped working. It will be remembered that it was in the 1980s that Ronald Reagan, the great communicator and voodoo economist, tripled the national debt and pursued improvident fiscal policies. Whatever the reason, this simple strategy no longer works. But it might be modified for the future if one were willing to do the research and give it the thought necessary. In fact, many commentators consider a 200-day moving average a sort of proxy for the Dow Theory. The fact that many so consider it is a point against it in my opinion, but that does not mean I ignore it.

Pluses and Minuses

Thus moving averages work very well in trending markets and not so well in sideways markets. Chartists have an advantage in dealing with moving averages as they can see when sideways markets develop without dependence on some blind numerical algorithm. The refinement of moving average systems is an advanced topic and further study on the subject is addressed in the Appendix on Further Study.

VOLUME ANALYSIS TOOLS

On-Balance Volume

On-balance volume (OBV) relates volume to price change. To get the figure, we add the day's volume to a cumulative total when the price closes up and subtract the day's volume from the total when the price closes down. The theoretical assumption is that OBV changes precede price changes, and that the indicator measures capital flowing into and out of an issue.

Other Volume Studies

Moving averages of volume may be constructed. A volume oscillator my be constructed by calculating a short-term and long-term moving average. When the short term rises above the long term, we would expect to see rising prices following the conventional theory of volume — that rising prices and rising volume are bullish, and rising prices and falling volume are bearish signs. Moderately declining prices with declining volume can be a bullish sign. Increasing volume and falling prices are ominous signs. However, it should be noted that volume interpretation can sometimes be a mysterious process and judgment must be exercised before believing any indicator.

Equivolume

Invented by Richard W. Arms, Equivolume is a clever graphic way of looking at volume.

Top of the box is volume high, the bottom the volume low. The width of the box is the normalized volume, which is obtained by dividing the volume for the period under consideration by total volume on the chart. The idea behind this indicator is that shares are more important than time in determining future direction. Arms says, "If the market wore a wristwatch, it would be divided into shares, not hours."

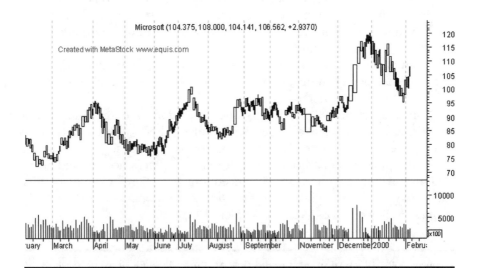

Diagram 17. Equivolume Graphic. Equivolume presents an interesting way of representing volume, as illustrated in this Equivolume chart of the ubiquitous Microsoft in yet another guise. If the market wore a wristwatch it would be ticking down to zero for Microsoft in this chart. This graphic form highlights the fact that after high-volume periods in Microsoft the price had a tendency to decline, a vivid lesson that Bill Gates has an infinite supply of stock to sell to his willing Windows fans. This might be called distribution under the cover of strength, as they used to talk about in the old days about X.

CANDLESTICKS

There are more techniques in the technical analysis tool kit than bar charting and number-driven tools. Two other techniques of great interest are used by many analysts: candlestick charting and point-and-figure charting.

Candlestick charting is an ancient Japanese way of representing the standard price data. Because of its particular graphic characteristics and long experience with the method, candlestick chartists feel they are enabled to interpret graphic patterns to forecast prices. Since its introduction to American traders in the 1990s, it has attracted numerous followers and is in my opinion well worth study.

Briefly, a candlestick is formed by taking the standard price data — open high, low close — and drawing a graphic which has a body composed of the difference between the open and close prices (the real body) and a stick (or bar) (the upper or lower shadow) marking the high and low of price action (see Diagram 18 for an illustration). With the real body colored according to the direction of prices (white for up, black for down) interesting new dimensions are added to graphic analysis. Just as by the mere act of bar charting prices we bring order to price analysis, candlestick charting adds color and formations to our graphic analysis.

Based on the observations of generations of Japanese traders, certain patterns and formations are taken to indicate vital information about the nature of the market under study.

As an illustration of these concepts, see Chart 37, from Microsoft, using conventional bar charting, followed immediately by a candlestick chart (Chart 38) of the same data.

Numerous candlestick patterns and formations are recognized and purport to have predictive value. But the method is not discussed extensively here. Rather, the reader should be advised that candlestick charting is not the philosopher's stone either. It requires experience and judgment and use within a sound and balanced practice. Further study of this interesting method might start with *Japanese Candlestick Charting Techniques* by Steve Nison (New York: Merrill Lynch).

Diagram 18. Illustration of Candlestick Method. This fascinating method of charting and analysis recently arrived (10 or 15 years ago) in the United States but dates to ancient markets in Japan. Another thing we have to learn from the Japanese. Bullish sticks are white, resulting from a market that opens on a low price and closes higher. The bearish stick is the opposite and is black. The "shadow" is the line above or below the "body." Patterns, or combinations of these basic designs, are presumed by candlestick chartists to have diagnostic power in analyzing the markets. The bullish engulfing line and or hammer are bullish if found

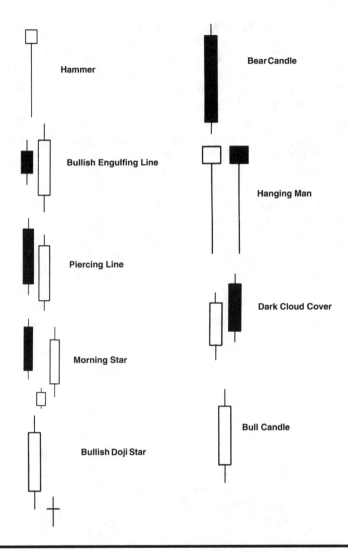

Diagram 18. (continued) after an extended downtrend. The morning star signifies a potential bottom and may be white or black. The piercing line is bullish and is the opposite number to the dark cloud cover. It is the relationship of one day's close to the next which determines their significance. More than halfway into the body carries meaning for the candlestick analyst. The ominously named hanging man lines are bearish found after a significant uptrend. As may be seen, they quite graphically (pun intended) represent the tight range of open and close and dramatize the long range traversed by prices outside of the narrow open/close relationship. This selection of candlestick patterns is necessarily limited here and the interested reader should pursue the subject in Nison's work and other references at www.johnmageeta.com.

POINT-AND-FIGURE CHARTING

One school of chartists who have on occasion had marked success in the markets is the point-and-figure group. P&F charting (see Chart 42) is quite a different animal from other charting techniques. The horizontal axis is not used for time periods as on other charts. It does, however, mark changes in the direction of price with each new column noting a reversal of prices. The reader will note that Chart 39 provides a new representation of the information in Charts 37 and 38.

The P&F chart is constructed as a series of Xs and Os, each entry being a box and box size (i.e., price value) being a critical factor in construction of the chart. The X represents upward price movement, and the next up box is not marked until price has moved equal to or more than the value of the box. For example, if the box size is 1 point the box will not be marked on a half-point move. In addition to box size, a reversal value must be specified. Reversal will indicate the number of points of movement in the opposite direction to start a new column. If, for example, the reversal value is set to 3, then price must move 3 points in the opposite direction to start a new column, which, again by definition, will have three boxes immediately filled.

P&F chartists identify formations considered to be of predictive importance, as do other chartists. In Diagram 19, some top and bottom formations and triangle formation are produced. Numerous other formations are recognized by P&F chartists and the reader may pursue study of this important school with references found in the Appendix on Further Study.

Most popular technical analysis software packages switch easily among the various charting methods — from bar charting to candlestick or P&F among their other capabilities. An excellent way of learning the nuts and bolts of these methods is by taking a market with which the student is well acquainted in bar-charting format and studying the case in different graphic and number-driven formats (candlesticks, P&F, moving averages, etc.).

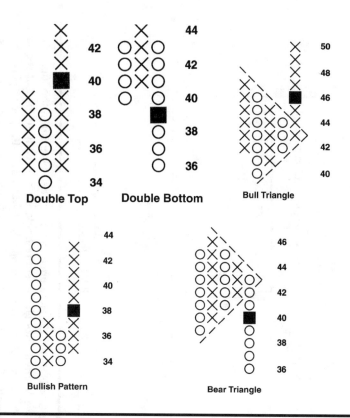

Diagram 19. Point-and-Figure Patterns. Variously reported to have been invented by Charles Dow and the Russians, point-and-figure (P&F) charting has its adherents, and it has been my experience that it can be an effective analytical method as I have known traders who were quite successful with it. The traders in question averred that they "optimized" the box size (i.e., studied the markets and adjusted the size of the box to fit the market, using, for example, 1.5 points or some such). This is, of course, the central question of P&F charting and makes it a quasi-natural rather than a pure "natural" system. Nonetheless, as is illustrated here, P&F analysts identify patterns in their data, just as chartists do. Double tops and double bottoms are illustrated, and the reader of this book by now will have no difficulty seeing in his mind's eye the pattern on a bar chart. The same is true for the symmetrical bullish and bearish triangles. There is much to be said for this method, whether or not boxes are optimized by sophisticated research. For those who have difficulty making sense of the bar chart, it might be a good alternative. The patterns illustrated here are, as might be imagined, the tip of the iceberg, and the interested reader is referred to Cohen, and Bassetti and Bassetti.

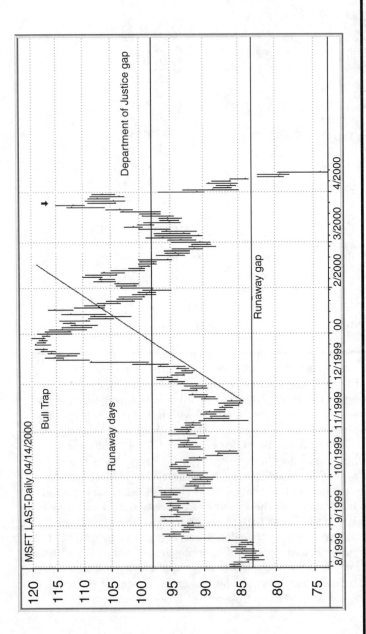

Chart 37. Microsoft, once more, to continue the case. See Charts 9 and 27. Here once again we see Microsoft at the top. Having considered the previous charts as well as the lessons we have learned through the entire book, we are ready to look at the same thing. But to see it differently. Now we know the end of the story, so this situation may be looked at with special perspective. Having examined the previous lessons on stop systems and methods we know that it was possible not to go down with Microsoft. *If only* we can separate ourselves from *belief.* In this chart and the two following charts we see the same data represented in three different modes: the bar chart, which should by now be second nature to us, and which should allow us to extend our knowledge to other forms of representation — that is, to candlesticks and point-and-figure.

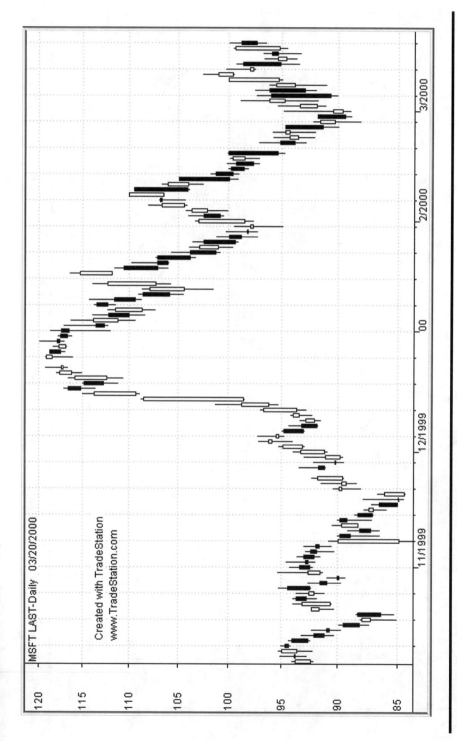

Chart 38.   Microsoft, Same Data, Charted With Candlestick Method.

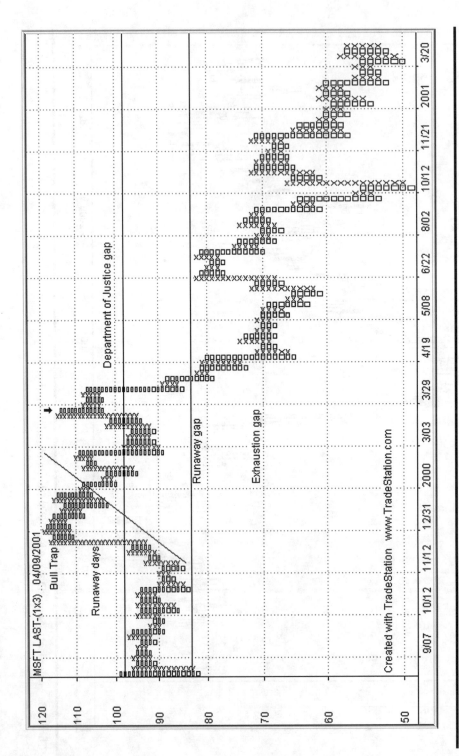

Chart 39. Microsoft, Same Data, Charted with Point-and-Figure Method.

WRAP-UP OF NUMBER-DRIVEN INDICATORS

Following, by necessity brief, is a summary of number-driven methods. But it will introduce the newcomer to the area and give him some idea of the possibilities and problems of this area of technical analysis. The reader will not have much difficulty in drawing the conclusion that the authors of this book prefer a qualitative experienced analysis to surrendering control of their trading to numbers. This prejudice should not unduly influence the reader. Each analyst or trader must find the tools and methods that work for him.

Trending tools worked marvelously well in the bull markets of the 1990s — trending tools of every nature, trend lines, support and resistance analysis, and moving averages. Studying this period once again reveals that old truth that anything including darts works in a huge bull market. Moving averages worked especially well for the Averages and, for example, Microsoft. In almost any kind of market, actually, I like to see a moving average line in addition to my own ruler drawn analysis. When the price begins to see saw back and forth across the moving average line, it forces me (if nothing else) to acknowledge a change in the nature of the trend. As an example, look at the Dow chart at the top of the bull market, Chart 34. This change of character then makes other number-driven tools more effective. Now tools which measure momentum and over-bought/oversold conditions become more effective. I personally would use stochastics and Billings Bands to complement a chart analysis in sideways markets, and there are those who do the opposite. Others hew to a strictly objective use of the tools. Many methods can be effective if combined with disciplined risk control.

For Larry Williams, a known trader in the commodities markets, %R has been a useful tool. (%R is a tool that measures overbought/oversold conditions.) Wilder is said to have done well with his tools. As I have said often, the inventor is the best user of his tool.

Generally it is my observation that a spectacular success in the market results from the felicitous combinations of trader, method, and market. Over the long term, smoother success is achieved by the robust method of Magee-type trend following, whether implemented with a ruler or a computer.

Fortunately, my readers are probably not well enough acquainted with the field to demand, "Where is the write up on Elliott Wave?! Where is the write up on Gann Angles?!" My easy answer is that those are advanced subjects — as well as being unnecessary for the general investor. Fascinating subjects for investigation and well worth it for the truly dedicated amateur or semi-pro, but out of place here.

V

CONSIDERATIONS FOR TRADERS/INVESTORS OF WHATEVER STRIPE— DAY TRADERS TO LONG-TERM INVESTORS

Implications of technical analysis are put in context for various kinds of traders/investors, from short-term traders to long-term investors: what kind of analysis is appropriate for whom. Sample trading plans for these various categories of traders are discussed.

There are the Marc Antony investors, sleek and well fed, who sleep well at night, and there are the Cassius traders, lean and hungry men who like a lot of action. To each his own, as Cato the Elder observed. It behooves the individual to know himself and conduct his investment affairs accordingly. Technical analysis has sufficient flexibility to be applied at any scale, from tick by tick real-time trading to dozing gents who wake up only when they get the call that the Dow has signaled a change of trend.

But. And. An awareness of the state of the market, its present rhythm, its direction and nature are indispensable to the survival and prosperity of the great majority of investors. In 1972, a group of the "best and brightest" Wall Street analysts chose a group of stocks that they said the investor could buy, throw in a drawer, and forget. Read further to see the results of this kind of fundamental analysis and "buy and hold" investing.

Keeping in mind several kinds of investors, Bassetti has proposed some sample trading plans for various investment types, which if followed might avoid long-term busts. No guarantees are ventured for day traders. Gamblers are directed to the nearest casino. Or, actually, Las Vegas is a happening place.

9

CONSIDERATIONS FOR SHORT-TERM TRADERS, SPECULATORS, AND MID- AND LONG-TERM INVESTORS

One of the more important aspects of self-knowledge is an individual's ability to recognize what kind of investor — or trader — he is. There is, as there is in most human activities, a spectrum of investment types. Diagram 20 is a little graphic that illustrates this spectrum.

An individual determines his character as an investor by his reaction to the seminal questions. How much risk do I want to take? How great a return do I want to make? How much activity does my personality need to stay interested? What sort of time frame is important to me? Once these questions have been answered he can look for the style of trading or investing that meets his financial and personality needs. In this process he should be aware of some interesting data from a table prepared by Professor Philippe Jorion from his book *Value at Risk*, which relates the probabilities of loss to the time money is invested in the market. Relating probable returns and probability of loss to time in the market, we observe the following: for an hour, the likely mean return is 0.0055% return and the probability of loss is 49.4%. For a year, the mean return is 11.1% and the probability of loss is 23.6%. The shorter term that one is in the market, the quicker the rhythm, the greater the quantity of transactions — the greater the likelihood of loss — from transaction expenses even if profits are realized on operations.

There is an exception to this rule. Market makers and stock market specialists make hundreds if not thousands of transactions in a day. They,

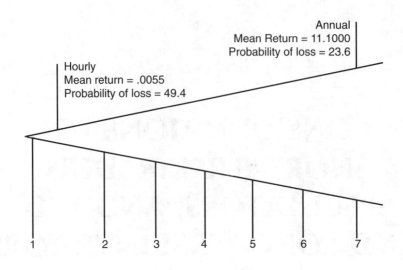

Hourly
Mean return = .0055
Probability of loss = 49.4

Annual
Mean Return = 11.1000
Probability of loss = 23.6

Diagram 20.   A Spectrum of Investors (Nonprofessional). 1. Gambler. 2. Day Trader. 3. Interweek Trader. 4. Midterm Speculator. 5. Mutual Fund Investor. 6. Trend Speculator. 7. Annual Investor. With this clever graphic I attempt to represent the spectrum of human experience in approach to the markets and investing. As the cone expands, so the probability of success increases. I see this spectrum as running from those with little or no chance of success to those virtually assured of success. This spectrum runs from the compulsive gambler at the narrow end to the long-term investor at the broad end. But, "What price glory, Captain?" or, perhaps, what is success? First of all, survival is success, as Gerald Loeb implied in his classic book, *The Battle for Investment Survival.* We have a counterpoint to this philosophy in the term "gambler's ruin," meaning the total loss of capital ending the ability to play. But is there a benchmark or measure for quantifying success? Indeed there is. The average return over 1 year in the stock market is 11.1%. Not much of a return the average speculator will say, and the inexperienced newcomer will sniff and point out the 90% returns achieved by mutual funds in the late 1990s. After the turn of the century and the millennium those same funds gave back much if not all of that profit. And anyway, only about 20% of mutual funds consistently beat the market averages.

But let us take the extreme long term: $100 invested in the Dow in 1897 would have been worth $39,685.03 at the top of the market in 2000. (*Note:* this is capital appreciation only. Dividends not included.) Not much of a return one would think, 6.017% compound interest rate annualized. Of course, that was the pathologically somnolent investor. The Dow Theory investor had, instead, $362,212.97 (*no* dividends). A bit better, or 8.366% compound interest rate annualized. Not bad. During that time how many "long-term investors" with short-term vision put all their money in the New Haven and lost it all? Meanwhile Magee, the mid-term speculator was realizing even greater percentage gains.

however, enjoy advantages the off-floor trader/investor does not have. That is, they buy on the bid and sell on the ask, the opposite from the nonprivileged investor, and they also pay negligible transaction costs — not to mention numerous other advantages not listed here. In addition, they are actually more businessmen than investors. They are turning over their inventory. Also, they are, in general, preternaturally skilled at their trade.

Lurking over all Magee's writings is the leftover Victorian idea of that old clubman smoking his cigar and telling his heirs "not to sell the New Haven" — the solid man who "bought good stocks" and required that "a good dividend be paid," and who tied up the New Haven in a trust which his heirs could not break after his death until the New Haven stock became worthless.

There are today's investors, like Warren Buffet, whose time frame is decades and who placidly take 50 or 60% market moves against their positions. Probably not all their positions. They are of course not strictly stock traders, but financiers who instead of buying the stock buy the company. Also, they are concerned with the value of their companies, not the value of the stock. Two different animals, "stock" and "company," as Magee has pointed out.

INVESTMENT CHARACTER AND NATURE OF MARKET OPERATIONS

Investors and traders will define themselves along several criteria: their choice of time frame, the rhythm and frequency of their trading, their profit goals, their risk constraints, their methodology, and their choice of trading instrument.

It behooves the newcomer to know himself well enough that he does not buy Palm on the IPO day thinking that he is a conservative investor. Nor will the speculator buy utilities. He might short them, seeing the mess

---

Diagram 20. (continued)   Each person must place himself on this spectrum, either through deliberate discipline and choice or as a matter of natural temperament. Identity is style, or vice versa. And the individual must recognize his nature — day trader or long-term investor — and fit that nature to the markets in terms of the instruments he trades, the rhythm he follows, and the tools he uses. The obvious prejudice of the authors of this book is for the midterm speculator, as Magee called himself, but each person must find his own identity — not just in life, but in the markets.

that the utility companies have made of energy deregulation and their feckless investments in nuclear energy. Conservative investors will not speculate in pork bellies, and their use of options and futures will be of an insurance hedging nature.

In the next chapter I suggest some hypothetical trading plans for different species of traders/investors.

10

SOME HYPOTHETICAL GENERAL TRADING PLANS

Here are some potential trading plans for various types, from gamblers to the long-term investor.

GAMBLERS

There is no satisfactory trading plan for gamblers. They are, in fact, best off in casinos where they can lose their money in a stimulating atmosphere with good music and amusing comedians and cheap food. Professional gamblers are not really gamblers. They are businessmen who like to take easy money from gamblers.

TRADERS AND DAY TRADERS

This is the fast lane of trading, actually not quite as fast as market making but fast enough for most people. Successful day-trading programs, if such exist, are primarily built on recognizing and instantly reacting to market developments. For example, one might see a stock open with unusual volume on a gap and jump on it, watching it in real time and stopping it just as we have discussed in Chapter 5. I have not previously discussed another type of stop, nor do I here. I will mention, however, for the reader's future investigation target stops and stopping on strength, so my reader who is a potential day trader will at least know of the existence of this kind of stop. Thus, day trading, or short-term trading, is primarily a matter of recognizing momentum and being on the right side of it.

I think there is a better way to day trade. If I were a short-term trader, I would recognize and trade the important daily patterns. An associate of mine does this profitably with key reversal patterns (*see Chart 26*). Also, at the top of the Clinton–Gore bull market, it was possible to lay a trap for stocks that were shortly to report earnings by going short and profiting from the exaggerated drops that occurred when they missed their earnings by a penny (*see Chart 25*).

Of all the aspects of long-term trading or investing we have discussed, risk control and diversification should be observed by the short-term trader or he will quickly be in a different occupation.

SHORT- AND MEDIUM-TERM SPECULATORS

The mid-term speculator will weight his portfolio more to the explosive issues — at the millennium the Internets and techs — following the mid-term trend-following techniques discussed in this book. He will also dedicate a part of his portfolio to the short-term trading opportunities discussed for traders. He will, of course, be trading long and short. The NASDAQ at the turn of the century was the primary medium for the speculator and could be played long and short, based on an MEI type of analysis. As this book goes to press, it is not yet clear what the next great speculative bubble will be — perhaps biotechs — but the alert speculator should be watching, and he should also be tracking carefully the NASDAQ so as to get long when all the blood has been squeezed from it. This can be determined by computing an MEI for the NASDAQ and buying when the percent strong stocks is below 8%, or, to be even more conservative, at 5%. (*See Case 24, Appendix A.*)

It was also, for example, merely a matter of common sense in 2000–2001 that the European Currency Unit — the Euro, which nose-dived from $1.15 to $.82 after its introduction — would come back to parity with the dollar. Those students in my graduate seminars who did not listen to this analysis are still paying their tuition with their own money. So currencies will always be good trading vehicles for speculators. In fact, currencies are one of the best trading vehicles, but that is the subject of a different lecture, for we are talking here about stocks.

LONG-TERM INVESTORS

A Simple Plan Following the Dow Theory

The simplest of all trading plans for the long-term investor might be to go with the Dow Theory. Buy the Dow on bull market signals; sell it on bear market signals. If a sporting type, sell it short on bear market signals.

Actually it is usually a good idea to confine shorts to a portfolio of individual issues, just as it is a good idea to buy the averages for long-term purposes. An average will hold up better than an individual stock, making the average better for buying purposes and the individual issue better for the short. How often, for example, do we see the Dow or S&P take a 1-day hit of 18% or 40%? Rare indeed, but at the turn of the millennium daily gaps of this type seemed amazingly frequent in stocks that reported a hiccup in their earnings.

This simple strategy may be endlessly varied. The more it is varied the less it becomes a long-term plan.

The Dow Theory plan was probably followed to some extent by those old-time investors who had the capital to buy the Dow. Today there is an easier way, namely, the Dow and the other major indices can be bought in small bites by buying the Amex ishares (symbols: DIA, SPY, QQQ). These unit shares in the Amex trusts allow the small investor (or even the big one) to trade the Dow like a stock for reasonable transaction costs. The development of these trading instruments is, in my opinion, one of the truly important events in modern markets.

Trading these instruments gives the investor instant diversification; participation in the most widely watched averages; downside protection as they and their components are in the portfolios of most important managers in the world; insulation against long-term deterioration (any buggy whip manufacturers will be ostracized from the index in good time by the index creators); high visibility (the most distracted investor cannot miss the highway and skyscraper tickers); and, as Magee would say, etc., etc., etc.

A Relatively Simple Plan for the Present-Day Mid- to Long-Term Investor

A perhaps more modern and practical plan for the present-day investor might be as follows:

1. Buy the ishares (Dow, S&P, NASDAQ) on breakouts, at the bottom of trading ranges on readings of the MEI in the 5% to 8% range.
2. Hedge using the stop methods described in Chapter 5 or when markets are blowing off or when 150-day moving average is violated.
3. Lift hedge when selling climax occurs or when long-term trend shows to have resumed or at bottom of trading range.
4. Never liquidate longs. Avoid taxes at all reasonable cost. Pay taxes on hedge profits when they occur.
5. When losses occur, take the maximum that can be charged off for tax purposes. Of course, take losses anytime rational methodology dictates, regardless of the tax situation.

OPTIONS AND FUTURES

An option is an instrument that gives the buyer of it the right to buy (a call) or sell (a put) the underlying security. For example, one may buy a call on IBM (or numerous other securities futures, indices, real estate, etc.). The buyer specifies a time frame and price at which he wishes to have this alternative and pays a premium to the seller. Or, for example, he might hedge his portfolio by buying a put. Thus, if he owned 100 shares of IBM at 100 and bought a put at 100 and IBM declined to 90, or 80, he could "put the shares" to the seller for 100, thus effectively insuring his portfolio against declines in the market.

If he owned ishares, he could do the same thing by selling a Dow-Jones Futures Contract on the Chicago Board of Trade (CBOT) to hedge his portfolio. A futures contract, unlike an option, obligates the buyer/seller to perform on the contract. If the price declines, he must, day to day, pay any losses incurred. On the option the entire risk is the premium paid.

The beginner must know of these markets and their possibilities, and he must also know that the options and futures markets are subjects for postgraduate study. Careless forays into these areas can be fatally expensive. For the investor who has done his homework, these are invaluable mechanisms. *The Appendix on Further Study* will direct the interested investor to the appropriate education.

ELEMENTS OF A TRADING PLAN

Regardless of where a trader/investor falls on the spectrum of time and risk, he should have an explicit and written trading plan. This plan should include the following elements. Specific numbers, securities, and percentages are for illustration only. Each investor should fill in the blanks for himself.

1. *Risk management rules.* For example, no more than 3% of capital may be risked on any one trade and, therefore, trade size must be adjusted up or down according to price and number of shares. No more than x% of capital will be at operational risk at any one time.
2. *Trade entry and exit rules.* Enter on breakouts, or on the first secondary reaction after a breakout, and exit on trendline break of greater than 3%.
3. *Capital management rules.* Portfolio will be diversified among 8 to 10 issues, or between S&P 500 and Dow; will be hedged by shorting weak stocks. No more than x% of capital will be allocated

to one issue, or capital will be allotted evenly to each issue (i.e., risk balanced).

4. *Trading instruments sought and permitted.* Being a long-term investor, trading vehicle of choice will be ishares, DIA, SPY, and QQQ for spice.

5. *Time frame intentions.* Time horizon of investment is 5 years, hedging on breaks of 3-month trendlines.

6. *Goals.* Profit goals are to track market performance on the upside and neutralize market performance on the downside.

7. *Portfolio analysis and review procedures.* Periodically (3 month, 6 month), the portfolio will be evaluated compiling statistics for profit per trade, loss per trade, volatility of instruments, etc.

8. *Tax plan.* Taxes will be paid on hedge profits. Long investments in ishares will be held indefinitely. Short-term needs for cash will be met by borrowing against the portfolio.

9. *Procedures to implement the foregoing.* Simply enough, the written rules for the foregoing — brokers, accounts, and so on.

10. *Shut-down procedures.* If the account declines by 50%, the accounts will be shut down and the capital turned over to an advisor or a mutual fund.

VI

TRADING IS ONLY HALF
SYSTEMS AND METHODS —
THE OTHER 90% IS MENTAL

Magee explores the philosophical and psychological aspects of stock market trading and investing.

A former staff member of Options Research Inc. was chosen as a trader in an elite commodity trading program (the Turtles). When he was trained by the principals only half of his training time was spent on systems. The other half was spent on psychological preparation.

In this section Magee establishes a firm philosophical and psychological basis for the practice of technical analysis.

The best system or methodology in the world is worthless if its user has no confidence in it. Thus the rational analysis of Magee's methodology and system is of primary importance. Beyond that, the cultivation of calm, poise, and, above all, planning for all eventualities prepares the investor for success in a viciously competitive area.

11

THE MENTAL SIDE AND THE PHILOSOPHICAL FOUNDATIONS*

Before anyone can use any method in business, or finance, or science, or any other field, and before he can judge properly the usefulness of the method, he should have some background of theory and the goals he hopes to reach. At this point we want to consider some of this important background.

We have already spoken of the use of charts simply as a record of stock prices and trading volume — in other words, the market action of the stock — and also of the convenience of recording other data on the chart itself rather than in separate notebooks or tables.

A more important use of the chart is in backchecking the results of one's judgment, building up a body of firsthand experience in a form that can be consulted and analyzed later, and in acquiring better perception — learning from both one's past successes and failures.

To many people the stock market is a confusing and confused melee in which prices move helter-skelter without rhyme or reason. But this confusion is, to some extent, a confusion in their own minds because they do not understand the complicated forces and the detail of procedure that actually cause stock prices to advance or decline. They might feel the same sense of meaningless movement that a visitor to a textile mill might feel the first time he saw the operation of an automatic loom. He might not understand at first sight that the strange shifts of the jacquard

---

* The alert reader will note here that some material has been repeated from earlier in the book. This is not an accident.

mechanism were not meaningless but were directed toward the orderly creation of a definite pattern in the cloth which would have meaning to anyone when he saw the finished product.

At the first or second lectures in a course, groups of students in technical analysis of stock trends are often skeptical as to the meaning or orderliness of the market. When they discover, as they do, that the long-term trends of stocks, covering a period of a number of years, show definite trends which often appear as straight line channels on semilogarithmic charting paper, they are likely to be overcome with enthusiasm, sometimes to the point at which it is necessary to warn them that the existence of trends, though true, is not the entire key to success in the stock market but merely one of a number of important facts that appear in the study of charts. In this field, "a little" knowledge can be a dangerous thing indeed.

THE PREDICTIVE VALUE OF CHARTS

The question, at this point, is, of course, whether the charts have predictive value — whether they can be of help in planning the purchase or sale of stocks with respect to the future movement of stock prices. We have a definite opinion that they do. But any investor planning to use charts in his own financial planning should understand as thoroughly as possible their theory and application. He should learn some of the characteristic behaviors of stock charts, check and verify what he has read and heard by his own current observations, and have some idea of what may be abstracted or surmised from a chart and with what degree of dependability.

Remember the gypsy shops set up in vacant stores along the second- or third-rate business streets of many of our cities. Today there is an empty store with a "For Rent" sign pasted in the window. Tomorrow the windows will be hung with printed cotton fabric; there will be displays in the window of the signs of the zodiac and various arcane symbols, and somewhere there is a display card announcing that Madame Zoloft or Princess Osira will read your character and that she sees the past, the present, and the future, clearly. If Madame Zoloft reveals the future to you, tells you that you will meet a dark woman, that you will come into a large sum of money, that you will travel across the water, this is prediction of the future. But not a very good prediction.

EVERYDAY PREDICTION

On the other hand, every one of us makes predictions involving the future every day of our lives. In fact, we depend on our ability to predict; we could not live or work without it. Whenever a man tells his wife he will be home for dinner at 6:30, he is predicting the future. Whenever he writes down the date of a convention, or trip, or theater party, he makes a prediction of the future. Whenever he enters into a business transaction, gets married, buys a home, purchases stock, he makes predictions; that is, he considers certain known facts, weighs and evaluates them, and arrives at some conclusions as to the probable (future) consequences of his decisions.

There is nothing mystical about the predicting process; there is nothing that automatically ensures that a man's predictions (or, as we say, judgments and evaluations) are wise or valid. They can be foolish, they can be based on false data or inadequate data, or obsolete data; the conclusions may not follow validly from the facts at hand.

But, the degree of a man's success will depend on his ability to abstract the relevant facts, to weigh them and determine their importance, and to arrive at the best decisions possible from the data available. The results of his past experiments and experience, if he relates these to future problems as they arise, constitute the background of understanding that we call intuition. If he is observant and uses each new experience to correct and add to the body of knowledge he has already, he will have, in effect, a cybernetic machine, a perceptual ability to continue learning and to correct his own methods, to improve accuracy, to update the basis of his premises, and to modify his predictions in line with changing conditions.

All this can be said in a single paragraph. But sound judgment, good intuition, foresight, and wisdom do not come about overnight by reading a book or adopting a method or discovering a formula. These invaluable assets on which our vital predictive processes in life are based constitute a whole lifelong process of self-education. It is not easy, but it is the only way.

THE LIMITATIONS OF PREDICTIVE METHODS

Not only is good predictive ability difficult, it is also not "absolute." When we choose a mate, or build a business, or buy a stock, we are making the best decisions we know how to with the best current evidence we can get. All we can hope for is to make the best choice of several in the light of the present situation. All we have to go on is what we have learned in the past. Our experiences with women will aid us in choosing the right wife. What we have learned about business will help in choosing the right products, the right location, the right kind of organization. And what we have learned from past experience about stocks will be our best guide as to buying the right stocks now. This is what is meant by good prediction.

If the conditions change, if new facts appear, it will be necessary to overhaul the prediction and alter it accordingly, or, in some cases, to reject it entirely and make a fresh start. Nothing in any prediction of the future is absolute or guarantees the outcome. But there is a vast difference in the degree of probability between Madame Zoloft's prediction of coming into a large sum of money and the weather bureau's prediction of a cold front moving into the New England area within the next 24 hours. The last prediction has a higher degree of probability. When the astronomers tell us that there will be a total eclipse of the sun on March 18, 1988, with totality lasting 3 minutes, and visibility in Sumatra, it is a prediction with a high degree of, if not perfect, probability.

In ordinary human affairs we do not need and cannot expect certainty in our judgments and evaluations. This is because the uncertainty principle is as much a part of living as life itself (which is also uncertain). Yet, with anything as uncertain as the duration of human life, the insurance companies make their actuarial tables on the basis of their past experience, and, because of the vast experience they have to draw on, these are, over the long pull, exceedingly accurate.

If we say, as we have said, and say once again here, that humility is the first and foremost need of a stock analyst, investor, or trader, this is not the kind of humility that hangs its head in shameful ignorance. Because a man admits he "does not know everything," it is not necessary for him also to confess that he "does not know anything." There are all shades of knowledge and experience, or the lack of them, between total ignorance and omniscience. If there is one factor that stands in the way of a reasonable and practical use of stock charts or any other market tool, it is the feeling that one must be completely right or one is completely wrong.

But, if a particular method, study, or point of view can do nothing more than improve one's total performance a bit on balance, then it is worthwhile. In fact, if it can aid a man in eliminating some of his worst habitual mistakes, it can be valuable indeed. It can greatly improve his "batting average."

As a prelude to any technical study of the market, it would be good for the serious student to do some reading in psychology, perception, general semantics, and so on (*see Resources for references*) to understand the workings of his own mind, so that he can see clearly what he is trying to do and how he can apply new knowledge and experience. This type of study should come first because most of the real tragedies of investment come about through (1) inadequate or obsolete information, (2) misevaluation of the information, (3) faulty conclusions from the data, and, perhaps most important, (4) stubborn habits of behavior that, like rigid prejudices, are often based on poorly conceived emotions and that often fly directly in the face of verifiable facts.

Also, in connection with prediction (or call it planning, judgment, foresight, etc.), it is a good idea to have some understanding of what kind of information and what kind of premise one will use as a basis.

Without any orderly, consistent program, it will not be possible to check back and see what the results of past actions have been in relation to the reasons on which we based our decisions.

One could say that the technical methods, like any method of prediction, involves looking at the past, checking whether the present conditions are greatly different, and, if so, making allowances for the differences, and then making certain conclusions, based on these studies, as to what seems most likely to happen in the future.

This is not a particularly mysterious process. Although in its details it may involve a tremendous amount of sheer labor, the principles involved are simple enough.

For example, if I have the past record of a series of numbers and the series runs as follows — 7, 7, 7, 7, 7, 7, 7, 7 — and the present term of the series is 7, I would predict, with some confidence, that the next (future) term will be 7.

If the past series runs 3, 4, 5, 6, 7, 8, 9, 10, and the present term of the series is 11, I would predict that the next term will be 12.

If the past series runs 3, 6, 11, 4, 48, 96, and the present term is 19, I would predict that the next term will be 384.

Depending on the total picture one has, one may look for a continuation of a constant number, or an arithmetic progression, a geometric progression, an exponential progression, a cyclic or wave-like rhythm, or any form that seems to fit the past and present facts, projected in the future, as if we were continuing some sort of "orderly" pattern.

The trick, of course, is to find the "orderly" pattern, which may not be a simple function but a combination of several quite different functions.

Also, one must be careful not to let one's enthusiasm run wild to a point where one "sees" patterns and rhythms where none actually exist.

And, of course, it is necessary to be on guard all the time against the various "pitfalls" we have discussed, the prejudices and attitudes that are so ingrained in us that they may distort our vision and "slant" our evaluation.

It is because these "ingrained" opinions are so deeply a part of our value systems that they can be so damaging if they are distorting our perception of the facts. That may be why it is almost impossible to "learn" stock trading or commodity trading solely from reading a book or attending a class. It requires days, weeks, months, sometimes years, of personal close observation and experience to implement the reading or the classroom study. It takes that time and that experience to revise the old and sometimes faulty concepts. For they are not going to erase themselves or amend themselves just on the strength of intellectual acceptance of a new viewpoint alone. The new ideas must be developed until they become the "habitual" responses.

One of the "old" tendencies that can be a dangerous pitfall is to predict in terms of a change in the major trend. This probably comes out of a whole complicated evaluation in which we appraise a stock according to certain "fundamental" facts about the company it represents. Such an attitude can lead to a frame of mind in which any considerable advance in the price of a stock leads to a certain habitual response, namely, that the stock is "overvalued" in the market. The conclusion, of course, is that eventually the stock will "find its true value" and the prediction from all of this will be that the stock should be sold.

The same situation in reverse occurs when a stock has declined sharply. The tendency is to feel that the stock "is priced too low," is "undervalued," "can't go much lower," etc. And these reactions lead to a prediction that the stock will shortly advance in price, and, therefore, it should be bought.

Sometimes this type of prediction (that the trend will reverse itself) will be confirmed in the future action of the stock. However, before pinning too much confidence on this particular method, one would be well advised to check the record of past predictions made on this basis. He may find that it is much harder than he thought to predict, even approximately, when or where the turning point will come.

I personally prefer to make exactly the opposite prediction. If I had only the choice of predicting a reversal of the major trend or a continuation of the major trend, I would have to choose the continuation. As Robert D. Edwards has put it, and I agree, "A trend should be assumed to continue in effect until such time as its reversal has been definitely signaled."

However, what we are talking about here is not the detail of prediction, not the application of technical methods; it is something much more basic: the limits of prediction. If we consider the question of whether the trend or direction of a stock's price should be predicted in the expectation of a reversal of the major trend, or in the expectation of a continuation, we will see that we are once again talking about an "either/or" situation. And, wherever we can, we try to frame the problem so that we can change the "either/or" into a matter of degree. Then we will be able to answer the question in several or many ways, and not in just two ways.

Sometimes, as in this case, we cannot exactly change the "either/or" question to one of degree, but we can do something that serves much the same purpose. We can reduce it to a "probability."

If you say BankAmerica is "going to go up," and I say BankAmerica is "going to go down," then in a month or after whatever time we agree on, you can take a look at it, and say, "You were right," or "I was right." If the stock has gone up you would be right, in this situation. And, if it has gone down I would be right.

And this, again, is the two-valued situation, the "either/or." Which is what we are trying to avoid.

You see, in this view, if your predictive method is "right" it will give you the "right" result. If the stock goes up in price, then you are "right," and your prediction is "right," and your predictive method is "right." But if the stock goes down, you are "wrong," your prediction is "wrong," and your predictive method is "wrong."

This leads to trouble. You might be quite "right" about BankAmerica this month. You might be "right" about Advanced Micro Devices next month, and about B.F. Goodrich the following month. But, sooner or later, you will be "wrong" on one. This, almost by definition, makes your method itself "wrong," at least in that particular case. It either discredits your method entirely or it casts a shadow and a doubt on it. At the very least, it destroys your confidence

Let me suggest here that we consider for a moment other kinds of prediction, outside the market. We will see how this same failure and demoralization can occur wherever we attempt to set up a "perfect" "either/or" predictive method.

But we do not have to do it in a two-valued, absolute way. We can recognize certain limits of predictive expectation in terms of probabilities, and then we will not continually be afraid to use our method because of our lack of confidence in it. We will not be expecting more from our method than we can reasonably hope for. And we will not be basing our method on a few accidental "successes."

Is this clear? It is clear that a stupid method of prediction (such as betting even money that one can draw a spade from an ordinary deck of cards) could at times produce a succession of "wins." If we see someone make such a bet over and over again, would we feel it was a "right" method of prediction, even if he won eight times in succession?

Or, to put it another way, suppose we were to have the chance of betting even money that we would not draw a spade from the deck. Every time we drew a heart, a diamond, or a club, we would win. Only when we drew a spade would we lose.

Under these conditions, if we were to lose several times in a row on this bet, would we discard our method as "wrong?" Would we reverse our method and bet that we would draw a spade, merely because of a run of luck against us?

Isn't it possible to say that, providing the deck of cards is an honest one, containing the usual cards and properly shuffled, it makes no difference how many times we "win" or how many times we "lose"? This does not affect the "rightness" or "wrongness" of our method of evaluation. And our best policy is to continue to use our evaluative method as long as we are convinced that it is based on adequate data and valid reasoning.

Of course, we know this. We know this from what we have previously abstracted from our experience in drawing cards from decks. It seems terribly redundant to have to go through this long discussion of something (perhaps an elephant stuck in our front entry) so obvious, so plain. We know that neither the roulette croupier nor the owners of the casino care very much whether we or any other player wins or loses. If the casino's bank is well-heeled, the "method of evaluation" will wear down the string of luck or the "system" of any roulette player, as every professional gambler knows.

And the method of evaluation used by the professional gambler is not based on being "absolutely right" on any particular play or series of plays but on a prediction as to the "most probable outcome of a long series of plays taken as a whole."

Then why is it that so many people either have no real evaluative method at all or follow one that represents so little firsthand checking and verifying that it may be worse than useless? Could it be that because they are so deeply trained in "either/or" and "right and wrong" they cannot habituate themselves to a method based on uncertainty?

If we know that on the basis of past experience and in view of the present outlook we may expect to "win seven times out of ten, in an even-money series of bets," we can accept this 7-out-of-10 probability as something akin to what would be a "measure" or "degree" in some other types of problem. With certain reservations and precautions we can accept this as the measure of our expectation, and by continually rechecking and verifying we can adjust and refine this until it becomes a highly dependable tool as long as the basic conditions of the contest do not change materially.

We can operate on this basis with considerable confidence. And, with this foundation for our confidence, we will not "need to be right" all the time.

Think what this means. Consider the nights we have lain awake and worried about what "the market" would do tomorrow, or whether "XYZ" would go up or down before the end of the week. We will not be able to eliminate all anxiety about the market, but we will be able to greatly reduce the amount of our tension and worry because we will not feel threatened with a "total failure" of our method every time a stock moves a point or so "against" us.

What we have done here is to set some limits on the predictive science. The average person seems to recognize no limits whatever. What they so often seek and insist on is an infallible method of reading the future. And they are so sure that if they only keep trying and searching they will come up with the "right" method, so sure that charlatans mulct them of millions of dollars every year by supplying spurious "perfect systems." (And this is also true on many other streets besides Wall Street.)

We have set limits. We have stopped short of the "100%" upper limit, representing infallibility, and we have set our goal considerably above the "0" of the thoroughly discouraged cynic who feels it is "all just luck."

By observing the results of a method as applied in the past, and noting the number of successes and failures, we can gauge the (past) success of the method. We can then project these results into the future as a probability and say, "I believe, on the basis of the past records, this method will probably produce an average net return of between 20% and 30% per year."

That statement is not nearly positive enough to satisfy the individual trained to think in absolute terms. Neither is the expected return anywhere near as large as such a person would expect (on the basis that he will "always be right"). Neither is it definite enough, for that person we are speaking of does not think in terms of "somewhere between." They want it right out plain and sharp.

Of course, the chances of our being "totally defeated" are much less than theirs. But, for them, it is necessary to "reach the top," and that means shooting at nothing short of perfection.

The novice in the market, as in other fields, is likely to shy away from anything "technical" and anything that he does not understand. He is likely to prefer what he considers a "common sense" approach, usually based on cause-and-effect reasoning. In other words, "this" will probably happen because of "that." The price of the stock will advance because of a coming merger and announced improvement in earnings, etc. This may be true at times, although the novice will also attach a great deal more certainty to his conclusions than a more experienced man and will tend to concentrate on a single fact or reason as the cause, overlooking the multitude of other conditions that can affect the outcome greatly. At best, he will probably consider only a few selected data and will not take into account the remaining factors, or he will attribute far more weight to his reasons than experience in these matters would substantiate.

Add to this the difficulty of evaluating the various products of a company, particularly when so many corporations today are widely diversified and may include many divisions engaged in entirely different fields. Sometimes the key to a situation may lie in the development of some new process or product by a hitherto obscure subsidiary. Often, it is possible to give several or many reasons why a stock should be behaving in a certain way. And it is possible that the most important reason behind a trend might be entirely overlooked. And in some cases, the real reasons might not be known or available to the public at all. This last could be the case when steps were being taken by some outside group to acquire control of a company in which a campaign for a change of management was building up.

On top of all these reasons why stock prices may move, there are also many others not directly connected with the business of the company represented by the stock — monetary changes, inflation and deflation, the general prosperity or depression of the country's economy, various political factors, and also the prevailing "psychological mood" of investors. At times investors generally are optimistic and have a feeling of confidence, and at times the investing public feels discouraged and is not much interested in stocks at any price. And there are times in which the market reflects only the general apathy.

Clearly, it is not possible to evaluate all these factors — many of them debatable, some unverifiable, and others intangible — by the same kind of methods one would use to analyze a chemical, balance a set of books, or measure a tract of land. The problem is not only vastly more complicated; it also means reducing to a common denominator matters of fact, matters of judgment, and matters of speculation as to the probable future course of things. On the basis of statistics, news, factual information, etc., it would not be possible for six men working independently to arrive at identical "values" for the stock of a company. Not unless, by common agreement, they all used a common formula agreed on in advance, omitting many of the debatable and unverifiable points, and then, of course, the values determined would not be independent and, in any case, would represent only the arbitrary valuations according to the rule or formula.

It is important to understand this. Otherwise, the daily chart means nothing, and, for that matter, the market itself means nothing. For if there were any complete and precise formulas for determining the value of a stock in dollars and cents, the democratic auction of the market itself would be meaningless whenever the market price did not coincide with the formula price.

But, from the practical angle of what we can get for a stock if we want to sell it, or what we will have to pay for it if we want to buy it, the market price is the valuation we have to accept. If a stock is selling at $50 a share and we and others feel it is worth less, or if we feel it probably will be worth less, or if we need to raise some money by selling stock, then, if enough people are selling enough stock, this supply will tend to bring the price down to $49, to $48, or lower, depending on the amount of stock offered and the urgency of the selling. On the other hand, if we should feel that this same stock is worth more than $50 or that it probably will be worth more, we would be buying it, and our bids would use up the supply of stock offered at $50 and we might have to pay $51, $52, or more.

Anyone has the right to feel that $50 is too high or too low a price for a stock. If an investor feels that $50 is too high a price to pay, he can bid $40 for it, but he will not get it as long as there are others willing to pay more. Or if he wants to sell but feels the price of $50 is too low, he can offer his stock at $60. But, here again, he will not get his price as long as there are others willing to sell for $50.

Thus, regardless of formulas and theories, ratios, and economic break-downs, the value of a stock, in terms of what we pay or what we get, is determined by what the investing public feels it should be. The price is the result of the bids and offers of all the investors: those who feel it should be higher and those who feel it should be lower.

It is easy to say, and many have said, that a price determined in this way by public auction may be unrealistic, that it might be the result of psychological forces — a wave of optimism, a spell of panic. It is true that if an investor had perfect insight and a complete understanding of a situation, he might set the value higher or lower than the market sets it. If he were right, and if things worked out as he anticipated, this would be highly profitable to him.

However, to set one's own opinion squarely against the judgment of the market calls for a degree of wisdom (or a degree of sheer folly) that few of us would claim. As far as the internal and corporate affairs of a company are concerned, there are officers and directors whose livelihood and business future depend on knowing their own company and its prospects. There are also employees, many of whom may also be investors in the company's stock, who are in a position, at least, to know more about what is going on than the outside stock trader. There are professional analysts and managers for large institutions — the banks, insurance companies, mutual funds, pension funds, etc. There are individual inves-tors who may have been studying a certain industry or a certain stock for many years. When a man tells us that a particular stock, selling now, say, at $50, is really worth $100, we should realize that he is expressing an opinion, his own judgment, and he is setting that judgment against the serious evaluation of other investors whose dollars are at stake in this evaluation.

If we seem to have wandered a considerable distance from discussion of the charts themselves, it is because this discussion is of paramount importance in understanding what it is that charts tell us, and why we do not insist that they not only tell us what is happening but also why it is happening.

To round out this section, one more important point must be covered. Clearly, whatever happens in the market to a stock reflects something that somebody thinks, feels, or believes will affect the future value of that stock: the record of past earnings or dividends on the assumption of a continuation of past performance or the projection of a past trend. Today's price for any stock reflects and includes all the hopes or fears anyone may have for its future. It is each man's opinion merged with the opinion of every other investor interested in the stock, and the resulting figure is the ultimate meeting point — "the bloodless verdict of the marketplace."

Thus, the market price at any time (which is what the chart gives us graphically) is a prediction of the future as seen through many eyes. It is the best educated guess of all those concerned.

But it should be clearly understood that although all of us have to make predictions as to the probable consequences and outcome of our action when we buy a house, when we get married, when we take a new job, or whatever we do, it is not possible to make these predictions "absolute." It might be someone's prediction that at five o'clock he would get his car at the parking lot and drive home in time for dinner. This might be a good and reasonable prediction of that future event. But it is possible for the conditions to change. The car might have a bad battery and might not start. There might be a highway tie-up that would prevent his getting home until very late. His wife might have sprained her ankle and gone to bed. We have to make predictions, the best we know how. But, we must be prepared, always, to change our plans and to make a new evaluation if the situation changes in some unexpected way.

This is a key point in the use of charts or in any investment planning. It is necessary to use the best current data we can get and to apply it in light of our experience to estimate the probable developments. But we must never become so "frozen" to today's opinion that we are unable to change it tomorrow if there is new evidence calling for "a revised map."

In discussion of the use of daily charts, we are assuming that the market price at any moment represents a meeting of bids and offers of those who want to buy and those who want to sell — therefore, the market value at that moment — and the chart provides a visual history of the market action in such a form that it is easy to see, at a glance, the trend of the stock's price and any important changes in price trend or in volume of trading. For such a chart, it is possible to draw some inferences and form some valid opinions as to the probable future market action. In other words, the chart is a tool; it is, in fact, merely a factual record, and its interpretation and use depend on the experience and judgment of the investor who is using it. Trends and patterns do not cause movements in the market. (We would question even the limited psychological effect they might have in influencing the trends of large and important stocks, because large and institutional holders of stocks cannot buy or liquidate heavily overnight, and among individual investors only a small percentage are willing or able to act on technical market action.)

VII

APPENDICES

A. Some Selected John Magee Letters

After basic training and drill the army enters the battle. How well does the theory and method hold up in the heat of combat? Appendix A presents a number of cases from real life and explores a number of cases from the experience of Magee's advisory company. About the only way that market wisdom can be transmitted is through the examination of particular cases from actual experience. Some students can even absorb these lessons without needing to directly experience the pain which opens one's eyes to being able to absorb the lessons.

B. Tekniplat Charting
C. Continuing Study Plan
D. Resources

Appendix A

SOME SELECTED JOHN MAGEE LETTERS

Section 5. Technical Questions — Stops

INTRODUCTION

For untold decades John Magee ran John Magee Inc., an investment advisory business which published a weekly letter commenting on the markets. In 1963, after learning some painful lessons firsthand in the markets and hitting the books (*Technical Analysis of Stock Trends*, 5th ed.) I became a client and subsequently student of this old-shoe, totally unpretentious master of the craft. I do not know how many wild and crazy phone calls he handled from me, but he was always the soul of a master who knows that he has a passionate and dedicated student on his hands. On my visits to him I was always impressed by the calmness of his office, the dry-as-dirt application to the business at hand — even when I tried to lure him into commodity trading in 1972.

Magee's letters were notable for their graphic elegance as well as their deep insight into the markets. It is obviously impossible to reproduce those letters in facsimile here, but Richard McDermott (the distinguished editor of the previous edition of this book) chose a sampling of those letters that I consider invaluable for the beginning (and sometimes the professional) trader.

I have supplemented these letters, or, as I have called them, cases, with some instances of my weekly letter which seem educational. Some of these letters read like new editions of cases from Magee.

The cases are organized into five sections and their contents are indicated by the section title.

Section 1

BENEFITS OF PROFESSIONAL MANAGEMENT

CASE 1

Benefits of Professional Management. From the Files of John Maggee Technical Analysis:: Delphic Options Research Ltd. www.johnmageeta.com.

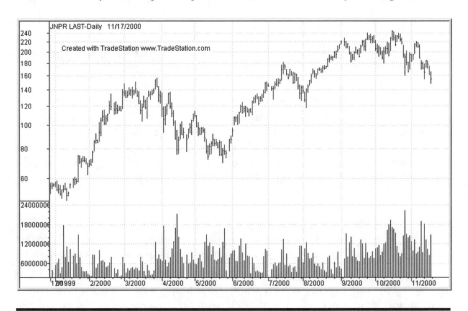

Chart 40. Anonymous. A Lesson for Quick Learners. The reader is invited to take ruler in hand, summon up the lessons he has learned so far, and decide whether he would buy or sell at this point. The name of the stock is kept anonymous for the moment in order to give the reader a chance to make a decision uninfluenced by hindsight. Make an analysis; make a decision; annotate your reasons for your decision and the outcome will be discussed hereafter. Do this before going to the next page.

Chart 41. Juniper, a Lesson for Mutual Fund Managers. Here is a continuation of the previous Chart 40. At this point the reader knows that the stock is a promising supplier of pickaxes, gold panning pans, and burros to the Internet gold rushers and, thus, as in the case of Levis, an infinitely better bet than the companies buying its equipment. Now would you buy the stock?

Here is an interesting case. During the great Clinton–Gore bull market many of my students — not to mention the rest of the world — gleefully jumped into stocks that had been "slammed" and realized good profits as those stocks quickly recovered their slammed losses. In seminars during that period I pointed out that this tactic would cease working when the market topped and that buying slammed stocks would be equivalent to jumping on the Titanic.

At this point in the stock's chart a prominent mutual fund manager enthused on the Yahoo finance site about the buying opportunity in Juniper. His enthusiasm was understandable, as he was a long-term holder of the stock, meaning he had already lost 50% from the top. I have deliberately concealed the manager and the name of his fund to protect him from scurrilous snickers of technical analysts.

Chart 42. Juniper, a Lesson for Mutual Fund Managers. The end of the story. Sad ending.

I quote here from my letter of November 24, written in response to that manager's buy recommendation and e-mailed to Yahoo and posted on my site at that time:

JUNIPER November 24 2000

There are those currently touting Juniper as a "buy." Technicians would be more likely to short it than buy it. Note the highest volume on the chart on the breakaway downside gap November the 21st. The gap and bounce three days later occur on negligible volume and look like short covering. Bounces of this sort (which are known in the trade as "dead cat bounces") are often followed by further price erosion, especially after plunges of such violence. Only the most adventurous (and perhaps rashest) of speculators would buy at this point and his stop would be the nearest low. The serious investor can find other less risky situations. And if he is set on Juniper patience is certainly in order until the downtrend has run its course.

Continuation of Case 1

It will be remembered that in Chapter 1 we talked about slammed stocks, or is a collapse a disaster or a buying opportunity? Here is the end of the

Juniper story. Sometimes a collapse is a buying opportunity. Sometimes it is an invitation to participate in disaster. Solid technicians are willing to exercise patience when the technical situation is dicey. Does it need saying that a fall out of bed on high volume is a dicey situation?

The reader will also find it instructive to read Magee's letter in Case 19.

CASE 2

The Best and the Brightest. Buy and Hold Investing.

In 1972 a group of the most prominent brokerage house analysts (fundamental) on Wall Street got together and picked out a group of stocks to buy and hold — to buy, throw in the drawer, and forget. The reader will easily imagine the reaction of Magee, myself, or any moderately competent technician to this proposition.

On the other hand, as John Kennedy's economist used to say, who could quarrel with the list of stocks they chose? A list of the bluest of the blue chips: Avon Products, Eastman Kodak, IBM, Polaroid, Sears Roebuck, Xerox. The reader should cast his mind back to 1972. No better blue chips existed than these regardless of what one might think of these stocks now.

Chart 43 shows what happened to IBM in 20 years. Chart 44 shows Xerox.

It would not be so bad if these two were exceptions to the blue-chip chosen portfolio. Unfortunately, this buy-and-hold strategy was a Titanic disaster. The table below shows the performance of the entire portfolio. Worst of all to a technician, the analysts chose these stocks at the top of the 1972 market. It does make one wonder about fundamental analysts. The reader will be amused to read Case 13, in connection with this case. Following are the results of investing with "the best and brightest."

Herewith a summary of the results of "one-decision investing."

Stock	Price 4/14/72	Price 12/31/92	Percent Change
Avon Products	61.00	27 69	(54.6)
Eastman Kodak	42.47	32.26	(24.0)
IBM	39.50	25.19	(36.2)
Polaroid	65.75	31.13	(52.7)
Sears Roebuck	21.67	17.13	(21.0)
Xerox	47.37	26.42	(44.2)

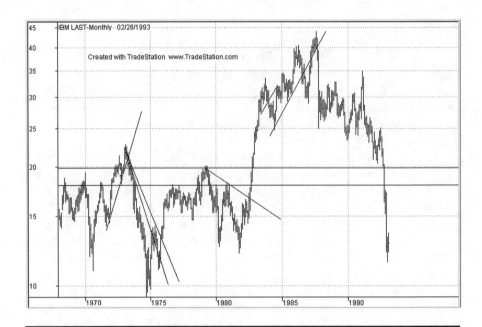

Chart 43. IBM, Best and Brightest. In 1972 a group of the "Best and Brightest" Wall Street analysts engaging in a drill which could only be described as a chance to get egg on your face (a panel on so-called One-Decision Investing) picked IBM as a stock to buy and put away. Twenty years later several smarter analysts reviewed their decision. The foolhardiness of this kind of methodology is amply demonstrated by the chart. First of all, the call was made at a market top in the stock — showing that even professionals can buy the top of markets. Second, no stop was set on the transaction, which resulted during the 20-year period in an immediate loss of more than 50% (in 1974). Some years later in October 1987, the analysts would have tasted sweet vindication seeing their recommendation double in value. Ah, but for too short a joyful time. October 19 came and went, and the top came and went, and after 20 years the one decision stock languished.

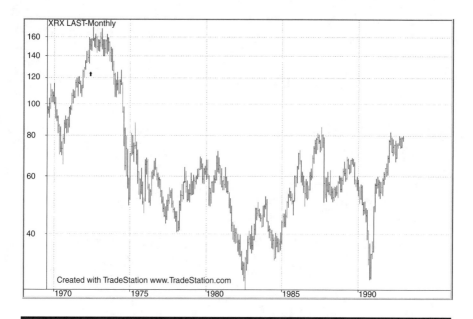

Chart 44. Xerox, Best and Brightest. Another example of those "Best and Brightest" analysts making a "one-decision investment." The decision in this case is especially ironic and painful because for the next 20 years Xerox never again regained the price at which those particular pundits had expressed their conventional wisdom. The lesson is clear: Believe the charts, not the experts.

Section 2

ANALYZING — TIMING — THE MARKET

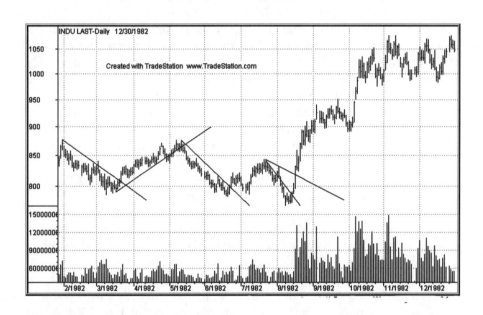

INDU LAST-Daily 12/30/1982

Created with TradeStation www.TradeStation.com

Chart 4.   From newsletter of August 21, 1982, the Dow.

CASE 3

August 21, 1982. Buying Panic (and What It Means)

Two records were set on Wall Street this week (*see Chart 4*). Both may endure for quite some time. On Tuesday, the Dow-Jones Industrial Average rose 38.81 points on near-record trading of 92,860,000 shares, the largest single-day advance in history. On Wednesday, an astounding total of 132.7 million shares traded hands, easily passing the 100-million-share milestone, as the Dow-Jones Industrial Averages (DJIA) retreated 1.81 points.

Tuesday's advance, a classical "buying panic," was front-page news across the country. Economists and business experts were called on to comment on the reasons for the upsurge. The consensus was that revised, more optimistic interest rate forecasts by two noted bond market experts had set the rally off. Other observers suggested that improving fundamental trends had been under way in the capital markets for some time, and that Wall Street (as well as the two "experts") had simply become aware of that fact.

We have never cared much for analyzing the reasons behind this or that stock market move. A change in direction in Wall Street may be due to fundamental changes in the business environment, or to purely psychological causes. There may be one reason, or many reasons, for a specific move at a given time. We prefer to concentrate, instead, on analyzing the technical behavior of individual stocks monitored weekly by our staff and selecting those most attractive for purchase or short sale in accordance with the current position of the MEI.

What can we say at this time about this most extraordinary stock market behavior? Did Tuesday's cathartic 38.81-point DJIA advance constitute a major reversal in the direction of the stock market? A review of individual stock patterns suggests that the answer to this question is "no, almost certainly not." Numerous stocks, we would say almost the majority, rallied from within a point or less of their recent, intermediate-term downtrending lows. We are unaware of any technical case for describing such behavior as bottom-like. The proportion of stocks rated strong currently stands at a relatively low 18%. Single-day high-volume spikes alone do not constitute reversal patterns. In fact, the number of stocks that have formed valid, recognizable 3-week to 3-month (or longer) patterns which we customarily associate with reversals remains extremely low.

What has happened then, and what does it mean? First, Wall Street has been treated to a rally, the best one-day rally ever. Importantly, the brokerage industry functioned extremely well, handling the record-setting activity in an orderly, confidence-building way. Second, the lift-off in many stocks was great enough to constitute an important potential first leg of the bottom-forming process in many individual stocks. What is required individually (and collectively for the market as a whole) is a lower volume pullback to support, and a high-volume subsequent upmove through the interim highs set on Tuesday. Then (and only then) can we talk about a meaningful technical bottom being in place.

Perhaps Tuesday's 1-day rally is a straw in the wind. Certainly, the MEI is in clear-cut bullish territory. And certainly, the interest rate climate for equities has improved dramatically recently (see our letter, "Change in the

Wind?," page 1, August 7, 1982). If so, the number of strong-rated issues should begin to increase notably in the weeks and months ahead; profit opportunities among the numerous stocks off 50% or more from their highs will abound. In the meantime, some individual stocks continue to swim against the tide with classically developed bottoming patterns already in place. We continue to advocate the careful accumulation of these stocks with purchases spaced over time and protective limits honored if necessary. Experience has shown that these "early bloomers" are often the best gainers following sustained MEI readings within the bullish quartile.

CASE 4

September 4, 1982. Dangerous Spikes

During the recent stock market explosion, a common bottoming pattern has occurred which is anything but common, technically. Specifically, many stocks — just after piercing support and establishing a new trading low — have reversed direction dramatically to establish new interim trading highs, breaking through one or more levels of resistance in the process.

The three charts shown (in the original letter) are particularly dramatic examples of this unusual technical behavior. In the case of Allegheny Corporation, a new trading low of 35⅝ was reached early last month, easily exceeding previous important lows of 37¼ (July 1982) and 41⅛ (March, 1982) and confirming the downtrend then in force. Within 3 weeks, however, Y had soared to 43, decisively penetrating July resistance at 41⅞. The moves in American Express (35 to 46) and Western Union (25 to 34) showed similar disregard for classic bottoming behavior as well as for previous resistance levels.

These unique spike reversals from new lows to new highs show many similarities with the broadening, or "megaphone," patterns usually associated with major tops (see Edwards and Magee, *Technical Analysis of Stock Trends*, 8th ed.). Because successively lower lows are interspersed with progressively higher highs, these patterns inherently reflect price instability and increasing volatility. Stated another way, it is impossible to state technically whether such an issue is in a downtrend or an uptrend.

Despite the seeming attractiveness of such turn-on-a-dime stocks, we have avoided recommending these issues in recent weeks. Instead, more classic trendline reversals combined with traditional bottom formations have been favored. If we did find ourselves owning these spiking issues, we would be inclined to sell or sell short against the box at least half the position, or, as an alternative, to write covered calls at a strike price near or slightly below the current market price.

To the extent that these dramatic spike rallies reflect the enthusiastic reaction of investors to the recent sharp decline in interest rates, they may be regarded as a bullish signal of better times ahead. In selecting which stocks to buy now, however, we continue to favor those with the reversal patterns typically associated with the technical bottoming process.

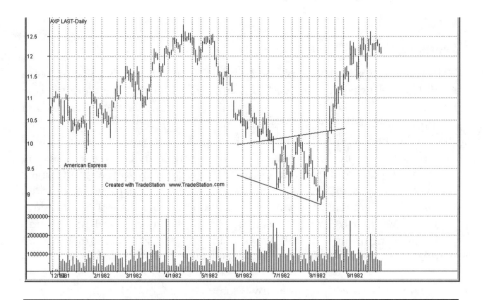

Chart 45. American Express, Bottom Spike.

CASE 5

February 19, 1983. Reflections

This week we were both pleased and honored to receive a copy of a small booklet titled *The Stock Market Innovators Survey*. We were pleased because the book contained a compilation of the investment strategies of 12 professionals "whose consistent success" supports the premise that "there are investment strategies and stock picking techniques which, albeit imperfect, vastly improve our ability to profit from buying and selling common stocks," and honored because our technical work at John Magee Inc. is the subject of one of the book's chapters. We particularly enjoyed reading the comments (reprinted here with the permission of the publisher) of William LeFevre, investment strategist, Purcell Graham & Company, Inc., regarding the inability of many investors to "recognize" a bull market — particularly in the early stages when one is upon them:

> The consensus opinion is always late to recognize the existence of a new Bull Market. In most cases, Bull Markets are not widely acknowledged until one third of the move has already occurred. This is infinitely understandable considering the emotional factors involved in investing in stocks, and the enormous influence of institutional investors in today's market. It takes time and some palpable proof of better times ahead before the fear created by a previous slide gives way to greed as the dominant emotion in the market. Recently burned, currently cautious. This is true of the institutions as well as the man on the street. Also, because of the sheer size of institutional investments — 70% or more of the total volume on the NYSE — it is even more difficult for them to reverse gears. Consequently, the chart pattern of a new Bull Market disguises a good deal of its momentum. In the early stages of a Bull Market, a DOW or S&P chart displays a saw-tooth pattern. Advances are often interrupted by declines. It is essential to note, however, that the market advances on increased volume and declines during periods of relatively inactive trading. Each advance and each decline takes the market to a point higher than the previous advance peak or trough. What's happening is that institutions, which missed the initial moves, are simply waiting for a correction before increasing their commitments. When they do jump in, volume spikes and the market moves higher. So, the moral of the story is that consensus opinion does not recognize a new Bull Market until its horns protrude far enough to "needle" the Bears into buying stocks.

We are reminded of the disbelievers who have recently been predicting a "100- to 150-point decline" in the DJIA, failing to acknowledge the significance of the recent move by the DJIA to new all-time highs after having been turned back at Dow 1000 or thereabouts for nearly 17 years (*see Chart 51*).

We have made the point often recently, and we make it again: Do not let the cries of these stock market Cassandras or the buildup of large profits in your investments make you so nervous that you sell out other-wise perfectly healthy positions. Evaluate each stock on its individual merits. Hold onto a position as long as it is technically strong. When it turns weak, sell it without fail. Leave the forecasting of the market's twists and turns to those who have more elegant crystal balls, many of whom have yet to recognize this bull market. Perhaps another upleg (or two) will finally "needle" them aboard also.

CASE 6

October 27, 1984. Calling the Turn: A Case of Missing the Point

Recently, we received a copy of an article "Calling the Turn," which appeared in the August 1984 issue of *Registered Representative Magazine*. Ordinarily, we pass over such reports, forecasts, predictions, and the like with only the briefest of glances. But in this one case we did hesitate, set aside the article, and attacked it with relish shortly thereafter. After all, "Calling The Turn" is a headline with universal appeal. And we are only human.

The article, it turns out, was really an optimistic assessment of the outlook for natural gas in the United States. "Are we at the Bottom of a classic commodity cycle in natural gas?" asks the subtitle. The author then proceeds to list a number of issues that suggest that, over the long term, a recovery in natural gas prices is likely. Typical of the points raised are that (1) "the depression in drilling activity means we're not replacing the reserves we're using," and (2) "production from existing gas wells is starting to decline very rapidly."

Although the author acknowledges that "natural gas prices are probably not going to get any Major, immediate boost from the crossover between supply and demand," he nevertheless advises registered representatives to approach their clients with confidence and simplicity: "I think we've identified a Major turnaround in the making, and it's got some great earnings potential for investors like you."

Now, our understanding of the meaning of "turning point," at least in the context of stocks and commodities, and the marketplaces in which they trade, is that point at which a change in the major direction or trend of price occurs. In our view, a recitation of trends affecting the price of a particular stock or commodity really has little or nothing to do with the issue of calling the turn of price itself.

A recent case in point, of course, is the behavior of interest rates in the United States. Certainly, major factors affecting the level of interest rates in the U.S. throughout 1984 were the strong United States economy and the huge federal deficit. We are aware of numerous economists and forecasters who based their predictions of further escalating interest rates on these underlying factors which to date remain in force. Yet, since June, there has been a major turning point in Treasury Bills (December 1984), and decline in interest rates, as Chart 46 illustrates.

We conclude that any article or prediction that heralds a turning point without specifically considering supply and demand as measured by price and trading activity in the marketplace is not worth the paper it is printed on. Or, stated another way, no pun intended, we think the authors of articles such as "Calling the Turn" have missed the point entirely.

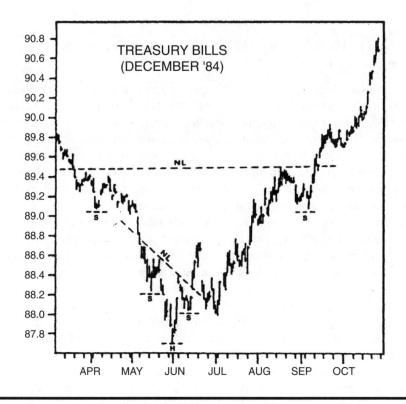

Chart 46. Treasury Bills. December 1984. The Turning Point.

CASE 7

February 1, 1986. We Would Not Want to Get Scared Out of the Market Too Soon

We note that a highly regarded colleague, a technician in fact, has likened the recent "widely publicized 52-point shakeout in the Dow Industrials" to "the stock market's performance in early 1946. In February of that year," he states, "the Dow Industrials declined…following that February 1946 shakeout, the Dow Industrials recovered by late May before beginning a 23% decline by the final quarter of 1946." He concludes, "I believe investors should be prepared for at least the type of declines witnessed in 1946, and on six occasions during the past two decades."

There is no doubt that riding herd on a portfolio of stocks, especially in an active and sharply advanced market, is a tense, nerve-wracking business. We have often noted that the owners of stocks that are going up in price rapidly seem to suffer more anxiety than the holders of stocks that are going down in a bear market. Apparently, the threat is mainly to the ego. It is always possible to rationalize holding a stock as it topples and slides to new lows. One can buy more of it, "average" the cost, accumulate stock at "bargain prices," and undoubtedly defend it loyally with optimistic predictions by the chairman of the board.

But when a stock is going up by leaps and bounds, the strain on its owner seems unbearable. To sell it after a 20-point rise…and then see it continue up another 20 points (like Union Carbide recently)…can hurt one's self-regard. And to hang onto it, and then have it crumble and sag and fall to pieces before one's eyes, can also hurt (like Storage Technology last year).

Thus, it is no wonder that there are so many worried-looking people pacing up and down at the back of boardrooms these days. They are the investors who happen to be holding one or more profitable stocks which have advanced at a rapid clip and in which they are holding a substantial profit.

It might be easier on the nerves, and, ultimately, on the pocketbook, if these investors faced the question as a problem in probabilities. They might ask whether there was any evidence to date that the particular stock was weakening, and whether this evidence was sufficient to justify selling it. Or, quite reasonably, after a big runup, decide to put a close stop order just below the previous day's close, to gain the benefit of any further straight-line advance, but to be safely out in case of the slightest reaction. This would mean, to be sure, sacrificing the ultimate hope of maximum long-term gains if the trend were interrupted by a normal period of reaction and then continued up. But it would represent a positive decision and, for some, it might be worth the possible loss of future profits to be "off the hook."

Or, the investor might continue to hold the stock through any "normal" reaction, until or unless it showed symptoms of a major reversal, and then sell it summarily. Although such an approach never captures the extreme of any move, holdings retained until a major reversal occurs often yield large capital gains.

Discomfort is a normal component of speculating, which is what all investment really is. Whichever investment approach one follows, it surely helps to understand the element of uncertainty which is part of the picture; and to realize that buy or sell decisions made on a stock-by-stock basis have a better chance of working out well than do dramatic across-the-board decisions to buy or sell all stocks because "the DJIA is about to go up (or down) 50 points."

CASE 8

January 24, 1987. The Elusive Crystal Ball

With the DJIA exploding into all-time new highs, we found this article written by John Magee nearly 25 years ago, still an appropriate comment on the often asked question, "How far do you think the market will go?"

THE ELUSIVE CRYSTAL BALL

A very good friend of ours, Carl Hamilton, teaches classes in technical analysis of stock trends. In the winter he teaches classes in Florida; in the summer, in New Jersey. He once wrote us concerning what he tells his students.

"I always tell them to sell at the top as they will then make so much more. When they ask me, 'What is the Top or how can one tell the Top?' I tell them, without smiling, 'When a stock does not go any higher, that is the Top.' When they ask me when do I expect the Top to be reached, I tell them, 'At exactly two o'clock this fall.'"

When somebody asks us what our "objective" is for a certain stock, or how long the rally is going to go, or whether the average is going to break 450, we are tempted to say, "Well, we're sort of handicapped right now. When Robin Davis took off for New Brunswick a couple of years ago, he took our crystal ball with him, and he never sent it back. So we don't really know for sure exactly what the market is going to do in the next six months."

You could say a silly question rates a silly answer, and we think some of these questions are silly. But we realize that investors are really very seriously concerned about this market now (or for that matter the market any time), and we are not indifferent or unsympathetic. But, as we have said before, there is a good deal of nonsense talked and written about the market, and a great deal of conversation goes back and forth across the board rooms, over the coffee tables, and around the cocktail lounges that really amounts to nothing, gets nowhere, settles no problems and means very little in terms of practical strategy and market planning.

The main reason we don't try to pinpoint objectives of time or extent of a move in the market, either for a single stock or for the average, is because the forces that will determine market action may be unknown or unpredictable today. Or, isn't it better to be watching the current situation, ready to change plans in order to cope with a new development, than to be chained with a self-imposed set of predictions that have to be defended to the last ditch? There is so much talk, so many words, that often seem to express only hope or desire, not much scientific observation. Sometimes it reminds one of the prediction that "Good old Centerville High will win, or lose, or tie.

Actually, it is hard to buy a stock on a breakout and then see it sell off on a reaction. It is hard to buy on a reaction and then sometimes see the stock go right on down to new lows. It is painful to sell short on a sharp down move which may prove to be a climax before a rally. Discouraging to wait and miss a fine opportunity altogether. These are the built-in sources of tension in the market, and the only way to handle them is to know that there are going to be disappointments, unpredictable moves, new events in the world that will call for a new look and perhaps for radically altered tactics.

In case you didn't know, we will tell you a secret. That crystal ball never did work very well. There are some good ways to operate in the market, we believe, but they don't depend on being able to "forecast the future" with absolute certainty and pinpoint accuracy.

Section 3

PORTFOLIOS

CASE 9

June 5, 1982. Managing Money

Let this be specific. We are thinking of a particular man whom we know. His name is not Kenneth Hudson, but he is a very real person.

Ken has been highly successful and has a fine business reputation. The value of his securities at the time we first talked with him amounted to something over $300,000, a loss of about $100,000 from cost. At that time he appeared very worried, quite unhappy. If he is still holding the stocks he held then, he is considerably more worried and considerably more unhappy today.

There can be no question as to Ken's competence in his chosen field. For many years he ran a difficult family business very profitably. When it came time to sell, he negotiated an excellent transaction, divided proceeds with several family members, and started another successful business. He is regarded as a man of superior abilities, high intelligence, and great determination.

However, a single look at his portfolio, or an hour of conversation with Ken, and one realizes that he is absolutely ignorant of the nature of his securities, has had no training or preparation in this area, has no feeling of self-assurance or confidence, and suffers a great deal of anxiety.

Just for openers, he owns 41 different stocks and bonds. Now there is such a thing as overconcentrating in a single stock, and there is a good deal to be said for having some diversification. But to follow the financial developments of 41 stocks and bonds at once is certainly beyond the abilities of anyone who is also working at a breakneck pace in his business or profession.

But there was more evidence of Ken's confusion. Within the common stock section of the portfolio, more than 50% of the holdings were in one industry And the holdings were unbalanced, ranging from as high as $30,000 in one issue to $3,000 in others.

Also the portfolio included not a harmonious but a seemingly random selection of ultraconservative stocks, "Go-Go" issues, more or less standard securities of average habits, over-the-counter items, and some esoteric stocks, apparently in companies in which Ken had friends, relatives, or other close "inside connections or information."

All this made it clear why Ken looked so worried and so unhappy. The investment program on which his retirement would depend was a mess. And this he probably knew. But he did not know what to do about it. Here he was, a brilliant and "successful" man with a considerable fortune. But in all the long years of his education, in courses which touched on economics, civics, and even finance, he had not had any definite instruction about stocks, bonds, the financial markets, and how they operate. And, like many others with a hardworking schedule and family responsibilities, he did not have the time or the energy to start the education he had never received.

There is a "gap" and a lack of relevance in the highly specialized education that prepares so many people so well for "making a living" as doctors, lawyers, engineers, or business executives but prepares them not at all to protect and to manage effectively the fruits of their life's work.

CASE 10

April 2, 1983. New Issues, High Technology, Wonder Stocks, and the Like

Recently, in one of our favorite daily financial publications, we read about "the return of the little guy" to the stock market. On the front page, there was the paving contractor from Chicago who dumped a considerable portion ($1,300) of his rainy day "nest egg" into 1000 shares of TechBomb (not its real name) at $1.25 per share. Before the day was over, his mother had invested $700 in the company and his younger brother $1,300. "It's like going to Las Vegas," he was quoted as saying. "Don't sit around worrying about it. Just do it."

The article went on to mention several other new issues, high technology, and wonder stocks which have captivated the public's imagination recently, often doubling or tripling in a short period. Not that all new issues or concept stocks are hot air, or close to it, or even that most of them are, but the enthusiasm generated by the current bull market, as with every bull market, is undoubtedly producing excesses particularly dangerous to the new or uninformed investor.

It all reminds us of a piece we wrote a year or so ago entitled "Hole-In-One." We noted at the time:

> No sane golfer would announce his or her intention of making a hole-in-one, this afternoon, on the next hole.... Although most people, consciously or unconsciously, realize that a hole-in-one is a combination of good golf and good luck, it is strange how many people go out to play a much tougher game than golf for the first time in their lives, set their ball up on the tee, whack it down the fairway or into the woods, and then wonder why they didn't make a hole-in-one. They go into the stock market on a gamble, tip, or rumor, staking savings they cannot afford to lose on the most speculative stocks, without diversification or predetermined loss limits.

> Champion golfers do not depend on holes-in-one or 'all or nothing' drives. Successful investors do not depend on hot tips and new issues to convert excessively margined, speculative positions to 'once in a lifetime' profits. Successful people depend on methods that can advance their interests in good times... and also protect their interests in hard times. Like bridge players making the most of the cards they hold, good or bad.

What really amazes us is that many of these new investors are buying stocks for which no previous price or volume data exist. Do they not know that when a company strikes a bargain to go public it invariably tries to obtain the best possible price for its shares? Only occasionally, very rarely, do stocks — especially new issues — double or triple in a matter of weeks or months. In times such as these, the established Edwards and Magee philosophy of trend following utilizing protective limits is of particular importance. Not flashy, perhaps, but rational, systematic, and time-tested over years of practical application.

Incidentally, the shares of TechBomb were last quoted at $1.12.

Section 4

LAUGHING AT THE PUNDITS

CASE 11

December 3, 1983. The Reason(s) for the Move

Rarely, if ever, do we feature the same chart in two consecutive editions of *Page One*. This week, however, the instant gratification from copper's breakaway explosion was simply too powerful to ignore. After leaping out of the potential reversal pattern on a 100-point gap on Monday, it advanced Wednesday to a high of 69.30 before retreating. For agile traders, the 300+ point, 3-day move was tantamount to a 75% profit per fully margined copper contract. Impressive gains were also posted by copper-related stocks such as Newmont Mining and Phelps-Dodge, as well as by other metal issues caught up in the storm.

We have no idea as to the reasons behind Monday's sudden explosion in copper. And we were more than a bit surprised (and amused) to read that it was all due to last week's great London gold robbery!

> The price of gold on international markets climbed $18 an ounce yesterday, to its highest level in more than a month, sparked by the weekend theft of three tons of bullion...
>
> "Currency Markets," *The New York Times*,
> November, 29, 1983.

> Copper on COMEX rose 135 to 125 points at the close in response to higher gold and silver prices.
>
> *The Journal of Commerce,* November 30, 1983.

And there you have it. The surge in copper was due to the work of a gang of London gold thieves!

Our own thought processes admittedly being somewhat slow, we are skeptical of the "reasons" for the gold (and copper) advances as reported in our favorite newspapers. With just a slight stretch of the imagination we could envision a happy group of suddenly wealthy thieves sitting around a cauldron, melting down their $37 million in ill-gotten gold, readying it for return to the marketplace. The result in our mind — little or no effect on supply and demand.

Our founder, John Magee, summarized his views on the reasons for market moves most eloquently:

> Every now and then some stock, a group of stocks, or the whole market, which has been lying dormant for weeks, suddenly takes off in a great explosion of activity.
>
> Some people will say, "Well, there must be a reason in back of this activity."
>
> It may be a good reason, it may be a bad reason, it may be a reason not directly related to the company, but perhaps to politics, international affairs, matters of control or merger of corporations, etc. There could be two reasons, three, many reasons, all true.
>
> We prefer to study carefully what is going on in the market, to make our inferences and decisions on that and not to dig too deeply into the rich, confusing veins, arguments, and hypotheses.

We couldn't agree more.

CASE 12

October 13, 1984. Which Way the Market, and Why

Everyone wants to know "which way the market will go." The trouble is, nobody really knows. Usually, there are numerous opinions as to the future course of stock prices, and just as numerous "theories" behind those opinions. From time to time, there is even a consensus — most of the "experts" who have an opinion agree. When that does happen, however, as often as not the exact opposite actually occurs.

Granted, forecasting the future of anything is difficult; in the stock market it is particularly so. In fact, so complex are the workings of the stock market that few "experts" can even agree on the reasons for market movements that have already occurred. Our favorite source of entertainment on this score is the stock market column that appears daily in just about every newspaper. Some recent examples follow.

On September 27, in the *Wall Street Journal*, we learned from the vice president of a major wire house: "Some institutions also were buying to get more stocks in their portfolios before the end of the quarter. Being invested was the way to look smart (to clients) this quarter," he said.

Only a week later in the same column, investors were advised by the senior vice president of the St. Louis office of another major brokerage firm: "The relatively low volume lately suggests that many institutional players also are sitting this market out. If you had a real fright in the market, you would see volumes of 120 million to 130 million plus. But we are merely in a lackluster market, and whenever volume dries up prices slide a bit."

If all this isn't crystal clear, perhaps the October 10 comments by the senior executive vice president of a very large wire house can clarify matters: "The market can't sustain a rally temporarily. The problem is that most money managers and the general public are either selling or sitting on the sidelines."

We couldn't agree more. Either the institutions are buying, sitting on their hands, or selling. That about exhausts the possibilities. True, stock market columns can make for good, relaxing entertainment, along with sports columns, TV and movie columns, and the like. But they certainly shouldn't be taken as gospel in a matter as serious as investing. As our founder John Magee noted more than 20 years ago:

> Every now and then some stock, a group of stocks, or the whole market, which has been lying dormant for weeks, suddenly takes off in a great explosion of activity.... Some people will say, "Well, there must be a reason in back of this activity." It may be a good reason, it may be a bad reason, it may be a

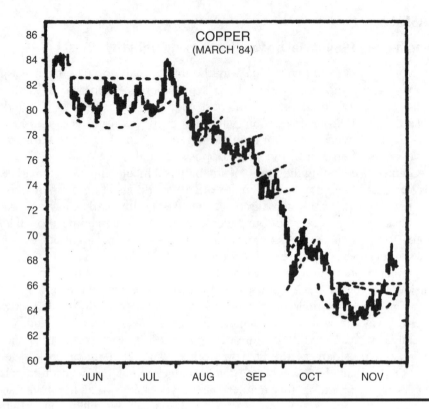

Chart 47. Copper. March 1984.

reason not directly related to the company, but perhaps to politics, international affairs, matters of control or merger of corporations, etc. There could be two reasons, three, many reasons, all true. We prefer to study carefully what is going on in the market, to make our inferences and decisions on that and not to dig too deeply into the rich, confusing veins, arguments, and hypotheses.

CASE 13

September 14, 1985. The Hemline Barometer and Other "Mood" Measures as Crystal Balls to the Future

> The market price reflects not only differing value opinions of many orthodox security appraisers, but also all the hopes and fears and guesses and moods, rational and irrational, of hundreds of potential buyers and sellers, as well as their needs and their resources — in total, factors which defy analysis and for which no statistics are obtainable, but which are nevertheless all synthesized, weighed and finally expressed in the one precise figure at which a buyer and seller get together and make a deal.
>
> *Technical Analysis of Stock Trends*,
> by Robert D. Edwards and John Magee

Followers of Edwards and Magee are familiar with the basic tenets of the pattern recognition school of technical analysis, particularly the hard-to-measure psychological bias which underlies the individual trader's decision-making process. Fundamentalists can argue about rational, fact-filled reasons to buy or sell. But clearly, the emotional state of the investing public is a major factor in the movement of the stock market. As chartists, we are constantly attempting to measure these changes with systematic analysis of price and volume. On a broader scale, however, an astute observer can also anticipate changes in the basic emotional foundation of the public by observing popular culture itself, a sort of "stepping back from the trees to look at the forest" approach.

Although this is not a new, or even a surprising, theory, we had not given the matter much thought — aside from a chuckle or two over using the "hemline" barometer as a measure of bullishness — until we read a recent article (*Barron's*, September 9, 1985) by Robert Prechter of Elliott Wave fame. Apparently, there is more than a shapely calf to meet the eye in hemlines and other changes in public taste. Indeed, Mr. Prechter postulates that popular art, fashion, and mores reflect the dominant public mood and that the stock market, being a highly reflective arena of emotional behavior, moves in concert with these major shifts in public attitude. He further suggests that these dominant moods, whether negative or positive, have a great deal to do with the character, and are possibly the cause of, historic events. "Major historic events that are often considered important to the future (i.e., economic activity, law-making, war) are not causes of change: they are the result of mass mood changes that have already occurred." If this is so, then one can argue, as Mr. Prechter does, that "evidence of mood change is the single most important area of discovery for those who wish to peek into the future of fundamental events. In the world of popular culture, 'trendsetters' and the avant-garde must be watched closely since their ideas are often an expression of the leading edge of public mood."

The article goes on to point out how fashion, movies, and, particularly, popular music tastes have signaled major turning points in the stock market over the past 35 years. These observations will not help a short- or intermediate-term trader much, nor will they aid investors in timing a specific stock position. But, as a broad measure of the general health of a long-term trend they have merit. Incidentally, by Prechter's reading of the popular culture barometer, we appear to be in a period akin to the mid-1920s.

For further information on this subject, we refer readers to New Classics Library, Inc., P.O. Box 1618, Gainesville, GA.

CASE 14

December 15, 1984. The Elliott Wave Theory: Perspective and Comments

This week we had the pleasure of attending the December meeting of the Market Technicians Association (MTANY) of New York.

Long-term subscribers will remember the MTANY as the organization which honored John Magee with its "Man of the Year" award in 1978. The speaker was Robert Prechter, publisher of "The Elliott Wave Theorist," an investment advisory which bases its forecasts on interpretations of R.N. Elliott's work on the stock market.

Of primary interest to Magee subscribers are Prechter's comments on technical analysis itself. The Elliott Wave Theory, it must be remembered, is really no more than a "catalog" of stock market price movements, laid one on top of the other, so to speak, until a grand, underlying and enduring pattern is observed; in short, pure *technical* analysis. Among Prechter's definitions and observations regarding fundamental analysis are the following:

1. First let's define "technical" versus "fundamental" data…technical data is that which is generated by the action of the market under study.

2. The main problem with fundamental analysis is that its indicators are removed from the market itself. The analyst assumes causality between external events and market movements, a concept which is almost certainly false. But, just as important, and less recognized, is that fundamental analysis almost always requires a *forecast of the fundamental data itself* before conclusions about the market are drawn. The analyst is then forced to take a second step in coming to a conclusion about how those forecasted events will affect the markets! Technicians have only one step to take, which gives them an edge right off the bat. Their main advantage is that they don't have to forecast their indicators.

3. What's worse, even the fundamentalists' second step is probably a process built on quicksand.… The most common application of fundamental analysis is estimating companies' earnings for both the current year and next year, and recommending stocks on that basis… And the record on that basis alone is very poor, as *Barron's* pointed out in a June 4 article, which showed that earnings estimates averaged 18% error in the thirty DJIA stocks for any year already

completed and 54% error for the year ahead. The weakest link, however, is the assumption that correct earnings estimates are a basis for choosing stock market winners. According to a table in the same Barron's article, a purchase of the ten DJIA stocks with the best earnings estimates would have produced a ten-year cumulative gain of 40.5%, while choosing the ten DJIA with the worst earnings estimates would have produced a whopping 142.5% gain.

We enjoyed Prechter's polished exposition of a technical approach different from our own. As for his observations about fundamental analysis, we simply could not agree more.

CASE 15

June 6, 1987. Earnings Forecasts: Dangerous to Your Financial Health!

A recent article in *Forbes*, "Upward Bias," asked the question, "Is it possible that analysts concoct future earnings to justify today's lofty stock prices?" The answer appears to be yes. In a group of 20 issues, which analysts were forecasting as the fastest-growing companies 2 years ago, the author showed that there was a whopping (surprise) error factor of minus 73%. This means the average earnings forecast for this group of stocks was 73% under the actual earnings result.

This got us to thinking about a significant peril in fundamental analysis which we read about a few years back in *Contrarian Investment Strategy*, by David Dreman. Dreman, in fact, was quoted in the *Forbes* article. Because it is clothed in presumably hard data, with an air of academic certainty, fundamental research reports are often taken as "gospel." Although Dreman is not an advocate of technical analysis, for the often-cited reason that academic evidence is lacking, his comments on the pitfalls in fundamental analysis were especially cogent and important when one considers how it dominates the decision-making process in the financial industry. According to Dreman, "Research has demonstrated that earnings and dividends are the most important determinants of stock prices over time. The core of fundamental analysis is, thus, the development of techniques that will estimate these factors accurately." But, he concludes, after looking at the record, "a system that appears eminently sensible in theory has proved exceptionally refractory in practice."

Without going into considerable detail in this article, we believe Dreman made a strong case for the argument that the root problem has to do with the fact that "there are very serious flaws in the analytical methods (of fundamental forecasting) that lead to consistent investment error." Briefly, the problem lies with man's information-processing capabilities. The human mind processes data in a linear manner. It moves from one point to the next in a "logical sequence." However, analyzing complex financial data requires the ability of the analysts to change the interpretation of any single piece of information depending on how he evaluates many other inputs. This is called configural reasoning and, from various tests on the subject, it appears that most of us just cannot do it very well.

Section 5

TECHNICAL QUESTIONS — STOPS

CASE 16

May 7, 1983. Beyond the Limits

Aside from wanting to know what's hot, or how far the DJIA will go up (or down), the most frequently asked questions we receive have to do with protective stop limits.

Most of the inquiries on the subject ask about a particular limit for a particular stock. Others, however, want a specific formula for limit placement. And a few suggest that we have substantially deviated from John Magee's methodology.

It is true that there has been a change in our method of setting limits over the past few years. John Magee wrote about using a formula based on a limit 5% under the last minor low, adjusted for volatility and stock price level (higher-priced issues make smaller percentage moves than lower-priced ones). The crux of this formula was a sensitivity index, but it did not prove to be particularly successful over the years and ultimately was discarded by the current staff.

However, as Magee wrote, "There is no perfect and absolutely satisfactory rule." We agree that a hard and fast formula is not practical. In general, our guideline for establishing protective stop limits is as follows. The initial or opening limit for a stock is placed at a point at which important support is evident (under a trading range or channel, under a major low, etc.). Most often, this will be a relatively wide limit reflecting several substantial support zones which have evolved in the basing pattern preceding our recommendation. An important objective of these initially wide opening limits is to provide every opportunity for a new recommendation to achieve its potential.

As a stock progresses in our favor, limits are advanced more aggressively. We specifically watch trendlines, minor lows, support-resistance points, and gaps. Especially important is the point that, if violated on a closing basis, indicates a change in the major trend. We refer those who wish to fine-tune the limit-setting process to include intraweekly limit adjustments to the section on progressive stop orders in *Technical Analysis of Stock Trends*, by Edwards and Magee).

We also use, on occasion, arbitrary "buy or sell at the market" exit orders. In particularly fast-moving situations (often after a merger announcement), in which straight-line advances (or declines) make the placement of protective stop order limit orders difficult or dangerous, this type of exit is advisable.

Whereas these general principles apply to perhaps 90% of protective limit-setting situations, there will always be that difficult 10% of the time when "the rules do not seem to apply." Consultation with our staff is recommended in such cases. In addition, subscribers may wish to trade against their open positions (i.e., sell part of a position on extraordinary strength, buy back on the pullback, or sell and repurchase covered calls), all within a period when no limit violation has taken place.

It is understood, of course, that protective stops under long stocks are never moved down, nor are protective stops over shorts ever moved up. Although we have modified our method of setting limits over the years, this fundamental principle of protective limits remains inviolate.

CASE 17

September 1, 1984. Big Money in Brain Surgery: Learn at Home this Quick, Easy Way

Some Wall Street wisdom is timeless. This commentary, written by John Magee on July 23, 1966, is as insightful today as it was 18 years ago.

It always fazes us a little to realize how many people spend so much time, money, and effort, apparently in a quest to discover the "hidden secrets" of the stock market. Mr. Average Man who has a few thousand dollars to invest and who may have a very keen understanding of his own business or profession, so often comes to Wall Street with the bright hope that he is going to find the magic word, or the crystal ball, or the unfailing oracle; a hope, by the way, that is not likely to be realized.

He will keep trying this formula or that "system" in much the same spirit that one might go out in the woods on a misty morning and peek behind every big rock along the way in the expectation that sooner or later he might find a leprechaun hiding there.

It is not that he is unwilling to put further effort or to spend money and time in his search. It is that he is searching in the wrong places for something that does not actually exist as he imagines it.

So often he is seeking something that will provide a degree of certainty that nobody can expect in this world. He does not realize that the market evaluation is a thing in flux, a day-to-day balance of the prospects for this stock or that stock, and these prospects can be influenced by conditions that cannot be predicted with certainty or, in some situations, cannot be predicted at all. Let a big contract be canceled, let a new "pocket war" break out somewhere, let any new circumstance come into the economy or into the affairs of a single company, and the market will revalue the stock accordingly. No method, scheme, or plan that we know of can anticipate everything that may happen in the future. The most that one can hope to accomplish is to estimate the reasonably expectable consequences of a set of presently known conditions. There remains a big area of uncertainty, and an essential part of the investor's problem is to recognize this, accept it, and understand that a considerable part of his strategy must be to learn how to cope with conditions when they do not work out as he had anticipated, or when new conditions result in new trends. He must learn not to make his original judgments "too absolute" and learn how to defend himself when they must be changed.

And, too, the new investor is often trying to reduce the market to a much-too-simple affair. He will cram his bookshelves and his desk with reports and data, stuff his head with figures, master a dozen rule-of-thumb "methods." He will have facts, sometimes too many irrelevant facts. And he may not realize that thousands of people are watching the market, studying it, analyzing it by various means, making their evaluations in their own ways, and some of these people have a great deal of insight plus a great deal of experience. They know what to do "if all goes well, according to rule," but they also know when "it is time to throw the book out the window" and improvise.

We believe that this ability to roll with the punch, to confront new or unexpected situations with courage and calmness, does not come from theory alone or facts alone but from deep awareness of both the mechanics and the psychology involved: a knowledge that usually comes hard, and is learned mostly in the "School of Hard Knocks." Like brain surgery, it is a matter not to be acquired in a few easy lessons but by actual experience and insight.

CASE 18

September 22, 1984. Forecasting: No Such Thing as a Sure Thing

Almost nightly we turn on the television (or call the weather number) to hear a rather pleasant fellow as he tells us about the low extending southward from Pennsylvania and extending as far west as the Mississippi; the Canadian cold front, now moving slowly southeastward at a speed of about 10 miles per hour; the relative humidity; present temperature at Logan Airport; and the small-craft warnings from Block Island to Long Island Sound. Also, that the next 2 days will be marked by much colder air moving into the area, and chances of precipitation are 3 out of 10.

To a good many people, this is either (1) the gospel or (2) the next best thing to it.

It is certainly not the gospel, however. There are competent men and women with long experience in the Weather Bureau, who are telling us what the probabilities seem to be at this time in light of their knowledge and the data before them. They would be the first to tell you that they do not know with certainty what the weather will be on Sunday, because winds can shift and new factors can come into the picture. But, taking it on balance, the predictions do represent an informed and intelligent "estimate" of what is most likely to happen. And yet there are some people who feel personally injured when rain appears at the picnic instead of the "sunny and clear" which was predicted, and they want to go down and take a swing at the poor, hard-working weatherman.

Sometimes a meteorological prediction is quite definite. The other night our friendly weatherman wrote on the board under chances of precipitation the figures 10/10, that is 10 chances out of 10, or "certainty." Actually, we did get some rain. But if you had pinned him down on that 10/10 prediction, he would undoubtedly have conceded that a more realistic figure might have been 95/100 or 98/100 — "close to" certainty but not "absolute." There is always a certain element of doubt, calling for tentative judgment. It is good to know what seems most likely to happen but always necessary to be prepared to revise a plan when and if data change.

In stocks, many investors are likely to accept the reports or data they may have as "final" and "absolute," the veritable "sure thing." But the stock that looked strong in August may run into trouble: a reduced dividend, a bad quarterly report, or whatever. And the weak-looking stock may turn around and start up. Operating successfully in an environment of uncertainty, however, is not "just a matter of luck." It is possible to make reasonable and good recommendations and decisions as long as one realizes that stocks, like the weather, are continually changing and call for the ability of an investor to change his or her mind when conditions call for it. In fact, there is no such thing as a sure thing. Consistent success requires constant monitoring of a stock's trend and the flexibility to recognize and take action if the trend changes.

CASE 19

March 16, 1985. When a Stock Collapses: Crisis or Opportunity?

In recent weeks, holders of several big-name technology stocks have been subjected to the agony of a "delayed opening – news pending" announcement followed by a severe decline in the market price of their shares. It all began 4 weeks ago when Data General announced that "current quarter earnings could be below expectations of Wall Street analysts" (from its Monday, February 11 closing price of 72⅞). DGN collapsed to an intraday low of 56½ before recovering to close at 58¾, off 14⅛ for the day.

On Tuesday of this week, holders of Wang Labs were subjected to a spine-chilling decline of approximately equal proportions, as were holders of Computervision (see Chart 48) on Wednesday when that company predicted "break-even results on less-than-expected sales" for the current quarter. For Wang, the drop amounted to 9⅜ points. The 1-day 9¾-point plunge in CVN (to 23⅞) amounted to an astounding $270 million reduction (one-third) of that company's market value.

Whereas the foregoing events constituted a crisis for existing holders of Data General, Wang, and Computervision, they represent an unfolding opportunity for the balance of the investing public. Just as computer and technology stocks were the "darlings" of the 1982–1983 stock market rally and are today its "black sheep," many of these issues will undoubtedly score large advances from current levels. In Wall Street, the wheel turns.

Technical analysis is unusually well-suited for such occasions. First, no technical tenet would justify bottom picking, or buying into a "decline" such as those currently under way in DGN, WANB, and CVN. Often such declines are precursors to substantial further declines. What technical analysis requires after such a jarring decline is a settling-down or cooling-off period. Typically, these last a minimum of 3 weeks and as long as several months. And typically, the bottoming process after such drastic declines involves a series of recognizable events — a rally of 30% to 50% of the preceding decline followed by a low-volume test of the "crisis" low. The final configuration of the basing process — head-and-shoulders, rectangle, or double bottom — cannot be ascertained in advance. One thing is clear, however; most of today's fallen angels will be available at current prices or lower for some time to come. And when the trend is about to reverse, that fact will be evident on the daily price and volume chart. Corporate announcements, as so clearly shown this week, simply do not occur in time to be useful for investor decision making.

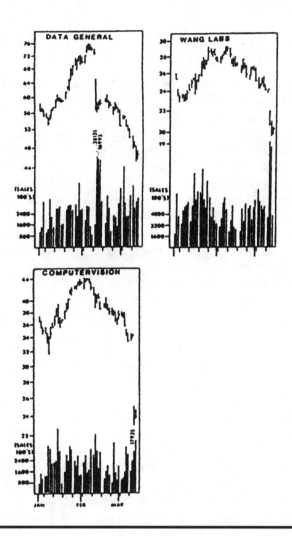

Chart 48. Computervision. Opportunity or Trap?

CASE 20

July 6, 1985. The First Shoe Drops

A few weeks back, at the invitation of *Barron's*, we penned an article about the classic technical pattern that often precedes corporate takeovers, or takeover-related activities. Entitled, "Worth a Thousand Words," the *Barron's* article (May 6, 1985) highlighted four companies "whose charts exhibit classic pre-takeover patterns but for which no takeover has (yet) been announced." The four companies were Allied Stores, Amerada Hess, Time, and United Brands.

When contacted by *Barron's*, spokesmen for Allied Stores, Time, and United Brands were quick to deny any knowledge about pending takeover or takeover-related activities. "We are not talking to anybody," said Orren Knauer, an Allied vice president. Time spokesman Louis Slovinsky reported that "the company isn't talking to any suitors," and that the company had "put in some anti-takeover provisions such as staggered election of directors." Even more specific was the spokeswoman for Carl Linder's American Financial Corporation which, according to *Barron's*, owned 58% of United Brands' stock. "There have been no talks either about buying the rest of the stock or about selling American Financial's stake," she declared. As for Amerada Hess, they failed to return a phone call from *Barron's*.

Imagine our surprise on Friday of this week, then, when a company called FMI Financial offered to buy 4 million shares of United Brands at 20. FMI Financial, the news release went on to say, is controlled by Carl Lindner, principal shareholder in both American Financial and United Brands.

Return for a moment to the United Brands chart shown in *Barron's*. To the date of the article, the United Brands chart contained "no less than five Friday spikes, an extraordinary number in our experience," we reported. Add to that the current offer to purchase 4 million shares made on July 5 — also a Friday! An astounding coincidence, we are sure.

We have often referred to technical analysis as the art of following footsteps on the charts. Price and volume data do reflect the activities of "informed players," as well as all others, and these often do provide unmistakable clues to impending events. Certainly, this was the case with United Brands. The jury is still out in the matters of Allied Stores, Amerada Hess, and Time. Which shoe will drop next?

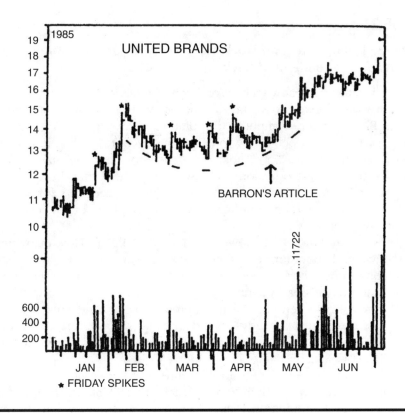

Chart 49. United Brands. Astute Chart Analysis Predicts Takeover.

CASE 21

July 13, 1985. Protecting Stock Market Profits, or a Trip Into the Wild Blue Yonder and Back

Except for the names (which have been changed), this is a true story about a woman investor we know who got wind of a big move coming up in Blue Yonder Computer Corporation. According to rumors, the company had developed a new process by which it could store the King James version of the Holy Bible on a memory chip the size of your eyelash, and major production was just around the corner. In June 1983, Linda High Hopes bought 2,000 shares of Blue Yonder stock for 80 cents each, or $1600; not an inordinate amount to place in an extremely speculative stock.

Those around the office, however, shook their heads. How many times had they heard about impressive new products, discoveries, or processes, all in connection with low-price (penny) stocks — only to see the bubble burst in the dawn's early light?

They were not even particularly impressed when Blue Yonder rose to $1.20 a share in July, a heady 50% advance in 30 days. They were even more impressed, moreover, when Linda called up and bought another 1000 shares at $1.25.

Their indifference turned to profound respect (and a little bit of envy) the following year when Blue Yonder reached $2.80, at which price their friend bought 2000 additional shares in June), and then when she purchased another 2000 shares in December at $4. By early this year Linda had accumulated 7,000 shares at an average cost of $2.46 per share. Her unrealized gain approached $30,000 this spring as Blue Yonder traded above $6 on the NASDAQ National Market.

Along the way, Linda's broker suggested she sell half her holdings (thereby getting her investment back plus a considerable gain), while "letting her profits run on the balance of the position." The advice was received politely but not acted on. And Blue Yonder, which had previously been something of an erratic performer, settled down into a long holding pattern at $6. Then in a short time, Blue Yonder sold off sharply, dropping to $3.60 a share where it again held briefly. No, Linda was not disturbed by this weakness, nor did she ask for quotes on a daily basis any longer. It had become a long-term holding.

Imagine everyone's surprise, however, when Linda's broker received a phone call to sell 7000 shares of Blue Yonder last week. We punched out BYON on the quote machine. It was selling for $1.20 per share! After some consultation, Linda decided to hold her shares a bit longer, not a bad decision based on their recent price of $1.80. Her loss, if she sold today, would be less than $5000 — not overly damaging in the world of high finance. But the foregone profits of nearly $30,000 are a great loss. To be successful as an investor, one must learn how to realize profits as well as how to protect against major losses.

In our service we have noted repeatedly that investors are continually subjected to information, rumors, and tips of every sort — most of them well intended — and that unless each investor develops his own philosophy with regard to buying and selling, he will be unable to operate successfully in the stock market. In the case of Linda High Hopes and Blue Yonder, simple maintenance of a daily chart, attention to trendlines, and a firm resolve to "get out of a stock once it turns weak" would have made all the difference.

CASE 22
December 20, 1986. Flags, Triangles, and River Sediment

What does the thickness of river sediments have to do with classic technical analysis? Quite a lot according to an interesting article in the December 1986 issue of *Technical Analysis of Stocks and Commodities*, one of the better monthly magazines devoted to the subject. The author, Curtis McKallip, Jr., is a consultant on risk analysis in oil exploration. McKallip wrote his master's thesis on the Markov transitions in river sediments of the Triassic age in East Central New Mexico (you would not need a sleeping pill if you had that tome by your bed). The statistical method used to measure the shifting sediments of the river is applied to equally "shifty" transitions between stock patterns as defined by *Technical Analysis of Stock Trends* by Robert D. Edwards and John Magee.

The pattern base for the study, which was titled "Investigating Chart Patterns Using Markov Analysis," was weekly prices of 19 commodities from 1970 to 1979. McKallip marked the obvious formations on his weekly charts, using the one that was best defined when one pattern enclosed another. Complex patterns, however, were broken into component parts; that is, the head-and-shoulders pattern was not measured as a unit but was considered a collection of trends, triangles, and flags. The article did include a long-term chart of wheat in which the various patterns were marked and identified. As a long-time practitioner of pattern recognition, we had problems with some of the author's chart interpretations and nomenclature. What he calls a symmetrical wedge, for instance, is a rectangle. Chartists, of course, will disagree on formations and our differences of opinion probably would not have altered McKallip's results.

Once the charts were marked up, the next step was to count the transitions from one pattern to another and use the data to set up a Markov matrix which uses chi-square calculations. McKallip has included in the article a two-page description of his methodology plus references (ours included).

This writer is not well grounded in statistical probability and has almost lost his ability to add or subtract without the use of a calculator. Therefore, I will not attempt to clarify a subject which is not clear to me. However, those with a mathematical frame of mind and access to a computer can obtain a copy of this magazine (for $8) from Technical Analysis, Inc., 9131 California Avenue SW, Seattle, WA 98136; (202) 938-0570; *now at www.traders.com*.

Without getting bogged down in the methodology, we can appreciate the results of the study. The total number of transitions tabulated in the article was 738. A number of them were too infrequent in the sample data to be of any statistical value; surprisingly, this included rectangles (symmetrical wedges). There were, however, three basic pattern groups that dominated the study: trends (we would call most of these up or down channels), flags (up and down), and triangles (symmetrical and asymmetrical). McKallip noted that "Symmetric Triangles seem to precede Uptrends but Asymmetric Triangles preceded Downtrends more significantly." His data shows a 64% probability that an uptrend will follow a symmetrical triangle, but his numbers for asymmetrical formations seem inconclusive to us. By far, the most significant transition pairs in the study concerned flags and trends. Over half (54%) of the transitions identified were either moving from a trend to a flag or a flag to a trend. The results of the analysis, however, were not surprising. The probability matrix showed that an up flag leads to a downtrend 66% of the time whereas a down flag transforms into an uptrend 77% of the time. In short, flags proved under Markov analysis to be highly valuable continuation patterns. Interestingly, the reverse was also true. Up flags evolved from downtrends 37% of the time and down flags had a 39% probability of forming from an uptrend.

CASE 23

January 17, 1987. Big Blue — From Bellwether to Bust!

International Business Machines has gone from a market leader to a laggard during the past year. Over the summer, while it had already slipped from its bellwether status in performance, it did, in fact, reflect the internal technical condition of the majority of issues then struggling along in a consolidation phase (see "Taking the Market's Temperature," June 21, 1986). But our "temperature gauge" metaphor for Big Blue faltered when new lows were consistently made during the second half of 1986 while the DJIA, and the majority of the market, were holding within consolidation boundaries. Indeed, the spark of fire that enticed us back into IBM in November has been reduced to a smolder following Wednesday's plunge through support. The breakdown was greatly aided, we might add, by *The Wall Street Journal's* redoubtable "Heard on the Street" column which contained, among a few distant bullish cries, the following pearls of bearish wisdom:

- "IBM is still a company that's not scared enough."
- "IBM's strong balance sheet is lily white and doing nobody any good."
- "Big Blue's critics now predict a horrible first quarter."
- "Even the company's most ardent admirers anticipate terrible news (for 4th quarter and year earnings)."
- "Some analysts now say net (4th quarter) earnings more likely plunged more than 40% to $2.55 a share — and perhaps fell even more."

It is no wonder a lot of bulls stampeded out of Big Blue this week.

Looking at this issue from a long-term point of view, however, suggests that IBM may be an excellent contrarian buy. On the daily chart, a well-defined downward-slanting channel has evolved since the May 1986 high. The lower boundary of this pattern is approximately 110. The long-term monthly chart, on the other hand, shows that a much broader upward-slanting channel dominated IBM from its 1974 low to the breakout of resistance in 1983. If the upper boundary line of this long-term channel is extended, it provides old resistance/new support around 110 during 1987; note the fine test of this line during the 1984 decline.

A line drawn from the 1952 low through the 1981 low crosses this year at (you guessed it) 110. We initially identified long-term support at the 1985 low of 118, and placed our stop limit at 115.

However, due to the intersection of the foregoing trendlines at 110, the limit in IBM is being lowered to 110 this week.

IBM LAST-Monthly 12/31/1987

Created with TradeStation www.TradeStation.com

Chart 50. IBM, 1975–1987. Testing a Thesis Based on Long-Term Trend Analysis.

We are not fundamentalists, and, perhaps, IBM's ills are terminal. But there are clearly some solid technical reasons to buy Big Blue during the current reaction notwithstanding the bearish comments in Wall Street. However, for those wishing to wait for a reversal, it would be wise to use a penetration of the downward-slanting channel at 132 to enter or add.

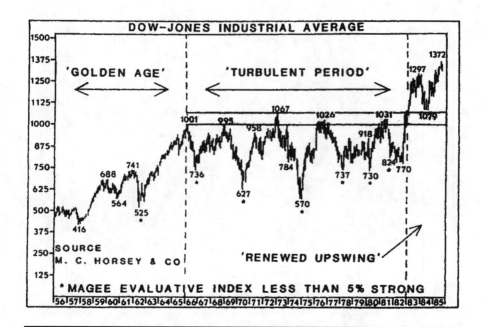

Chart 51. Dow-Jones, Illustration of Magee Evaluative Index.

CASE 24

September 28, 1985. An Oversold Market

This week, the MEI fell to 9% strong, its deepest penetration into the oversold quadrant this year. Not since June 1984 has this index been lower (see Chart 51). Shortly after its June low of 8% strong, the MEI headed steadily higher, giving an aggressive buy signal throughout late June and July.

The June 1984 MEI low of 8% strong, together with the 8% level reached on February 25, 1984, constituted a double bottom oversold reading for this index. It corresponded to the 1079 bottom recorded by the DJIA on June 18, 1984, after which that index advanced steadily to its recent July peak of 1372.

For more than 20 years, all major stock market bottoms have corresponded with extremely low MEI readings. During the "turbulent period," when the stock market oscillated violently but showed no gain at all, MEI readings of 5% strong or less corresponded with all major DJIA bottoms until the June 1982 low of 9% strong, which immediately preceded the stock market's upward explosion.

That slightly higher than "5% strong or less" bottom was an important clue that a reinvigorated stock market was at hand; the straight-line DJIA advance from 770 to nearly 1300 ended a 17-year "do-nothing" period for stock prices and ushered in the "renewed upswing" period shown on the chart.

In this context, the "8% strong bottom" of June 1984 and the current MEI reading of 9% strong take on added meaning. If, in fact, we are in a period of renewed (or major secular) upswing, stock market bottoms will tend to be less severe and tops more extremely overbought than would otherwise be the case. Both the June 1982 DJIA low and that of June 1984 fit this model. Because secular stock market waves tend to last for many years even decades, the likelihood is that the current MEI reading of 9% strong will also define a major DJIA low.

Appendix B

TEKNIPLAT CHARTING

The purpose of this discussion is to explain the nature of the bar chart, something of the history and development of the use of charts in the evaluation of securities, the philosophy and rationale of charting, some of the technical patterns seen on charts and their use and interpretation, methods and details of application and use, and comments and suggestions as to the setting up and maintaining of daily charts.

WHAT IS A BAR CHART?

A bar chart is one of the many methods of representing information in graphic form. It consists of a rectilinear grid on which two variables can be plotted. Thus, the vertical axis might be scaled to represent "miles per hour" of a moving automobile and the horizontal axis, the "rate of gasoline consumption." The vertical axis might be "total number of employees" in various industries and the horizontal axis "average wage of employees." In many kinds of engineering, sociological, and economic problems, the horizontal axis represents time (hours, days, months, etc.) and the vertical axis measures the magnitude of a second variable such as population, net income, pressure, or whatever data are under examination. In the study of securities, bar charts are widely used to show the record of price trends and fluctuations over a period. These charts can be adapted to any type of financial market: stocks, bonds, warrants, debentures, commodities, etc. They can be used for long periods, perhaps covering many years, or they may be focused down to short-term trends on a daily or even hourly basis.

In charting security prices, the high and low prices for the day (if it is a daily chart that is being run) are plotted on the line that represents the particular day, and the high and low are connected by a vertical line. Usually, the closing or last price for the day is shown as a cross-line on this vertical range. It is also possible to show both the opening price and the closing price, using a short line to the left of the vertical range for the opening and a short line to the right to indicate the close.

The volume of trading may be shown on a separate scale near the bottom of the sheet, directly under the vertical lines showing the daily price range. For weekly charts or monthly charts, the procedure is exactly the same except that each horizontal interval represents a week or a month instead of a day.

Because the horizontal scale on the chart provides a "calendar," it is possible to enter any other data in which one may be interested directly on the chart. This will include, of course, dividend or ex-distribution dates, the dates of stock splits, and any data that might seem important as to earnings, mergers, announcements of new products, etc. By noting on the proper date the purchase or sale of a stock and the price paid or received, investors will have a record of these transactions right on the chart; this will make it easy to check the status of a transaction, the profit or loss on it, and this record will serve as a valuable study later as to the degree of success of one's decisions.

CONSTRUCTION OF A DAILY CHART

A stock chart (daily, weekly, or monthly) ordinarily has a time scale running from left to right, covering the period included in the chart, and a vertical scale representing the price of the stock.

The horizontal time scale is of uniform intervals. But the vertical price scale may be on any of several scales. The chart can be made on ordinary cross-section paper, or on a chart sheet having arithmetic vertical divisions. In this case, the spacing is uniform from bottom to top, and the distance between 10 and 20 will be the same as the distance between 20 and 30, or between 80 and 90.

Or, the vertical scale may be on logarithmic, square root, cube root, or some other scale. In such cases, the scale will usually give a larger vertical distance to a lower-priced stock, and, as the price advances, the vertical scale becomes more compressed. Thus, the distance between 10 and 20 will be more than the distance between 20 and 30, and, again, this will be more than the distance between 80 and 90. The reason for using a scale which "shrinks" as the price advances is that, obviously, an advance of 5 points in a stock selling at $10 is much more important in its effect on capital than an advance of 5 points in a stock selling at $50. In the first case, the 5 points would represent a gain of 50%, in the second case, only 10%.

Because what we are concerned with is the percentage change in capital represented by a price move, there is a great deal to be said for using what is known as a percentage, ratio, or logarithmic scale. The characteristic of this scale is that it will measure percentage advances or deadlines directly,

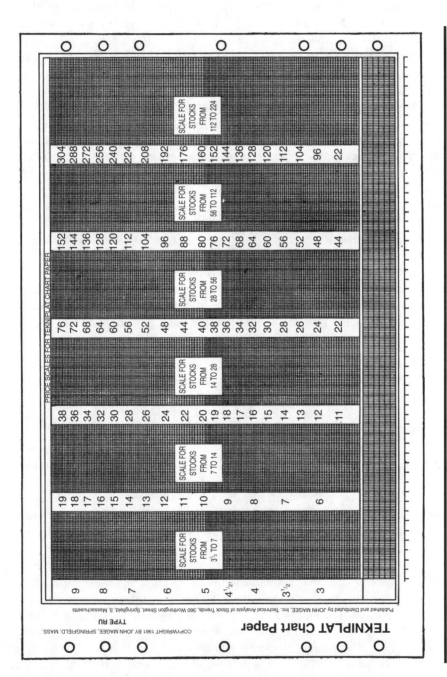

Chart 52. Tekniplat Paper.

and a move of 10% or 35%, or any other percentage, will always appear as the same vertical distance on the chart regardless of the price of the stock. Thus, chartwise, a move from $1000 a share to $1500 a share would look exactly like an advance from $10 to $15, or from $50 to $75; any advance of 50% in a stock would cover the same vertical distance. This makes it possible to compare the action of a stock with any other stock directly, or to compare the action of a stock with a group average, or to compare stocks or groups with general market averages similarly scaled.

The objection one sometimes hears about logarithmic charts is that the "squeezing" of the scale as the price advances makes it impossible to chart precisely to the last eighth when the price has moved up greatly. In other words, a move of ⅛ point will be shown plainly on stocks in the 10s and 20s but will not show precisely on stocks selling in the 100s. But, one should realize a move of ⅛ point is quite important, say, when a stock is selling at $5 a share, and is insignificant on one that is quoted at $150.

The other question new users bring up regarding the logarithmic scale is that continually "shrinking" intervals seems strange (at first) to them if they have been used to using plain cross-section paper (i.e., arithmetically scaled sheets). Actually, the changing log scale provides points of reference that the eye soon learns to recognize, and there is less chance of entering a price at the wrong place than when using paper that has a perfectly uniform scale.

HOW TO USE TEKNIPLAT CHART PAPER

If you have never kept charts on this type of paper, known as semilogarithmic, ratio, or proportion, these instructions will help you to read and understand the charts more easily, and they will help you in getting started if you are setting up charts of your own.

There will be no problem here for the engineer or the experienced chartist, but many people who have not kept charts before, or who are familiar only with the arithmetic price scale where the intervals are uniform throughout, may be puzzled at first by the continually changing vertical spaces. As you will discover, however, this very feature makes for easier and faster charting, because the various prices always lie at the same point in one of the "banks," and the eye becomes adept in placing the point needed automatically, without reference to the index figures along the left margin.

On many simple charts, showing hours of work, temperature changes, depth of water, etc., it is perfectly satisfactory to use ordinary cross-section paper, so that each hour, degree, or foot is represented by the same vertical distance on the chart. The difference between 5 feet and 10 feet is the same as the distance between 105 feet and 110 feet.

But this is not a good way to represent the differences in stock prices. It is perfectly true that the difference in market value between a stock selling at $5 a share and one selling at $10 a share is $5, or $500 on a block of 100 shares, and that the difference between the value of a stock selling at $100 and one at $105 is also $5, or $500 on a block of 100 shares. But, in this latter case, there is a great deal more capital involved.

For example, if you put $1000 into a stock at $5, you would get (disregarding commission) 200 shares. And if you sold these at $10, you would receive $2000. You would have a profit of $1000, or 100%. But, if you put your $1000 into a stock selling at $105, you would be able to buy only 9 shares And when you sold 5 points higher at $110, your profit would be only $45 or 4.5%.

It will give you a better comparison of the percentages of profit in various stock transactions if the price scale of your chart is designed to show equal percentages of advance or decline as equal vertical distances, regardless of the price of the stock. This is exactly what the Tekniplat charting paper does. A certain vertical distance on the paper will always indicate the same percentage change, and a trend moving at a certain angle will always indicate the same rate of percentage change, no matter what the price of the stock may be.

Clearly, one point of advance or decline is much more important to you in a stock selling at $5 or $6 a share than in one selling at $100. Thus it should not surprise you that the interval between $5 and $6 is much larger than that between $100 and $101. And, because the stocks at lower prices make larger percentage moves for each point, or half point, or one-eighth point, these moves will show up more plainly on their charts Actually, it is not possible on the Tekniplat paper to show a single eighth of change for a stock selling as high as $100. But this is just another way of saying that a single eighth is not important at that price. You might well be concerned about the difference between 1¼ and 1⅜. But you would not care too much whether you sold at 103 or 103⅛.

Because all your stocks will be plotted on a proportional basis, you can compare directly the action of any one stock with any other as to pattern, trend, etc. Thus, a stock selling at $16 can be compared with a stock selling at $56. However, although the percentage moves will be strictly comparable, it should be pointed out that, typically, the high-priced issues make smaller percentage moves than the low-priced ones.

The Price Scale

The price scale on Tekniplat paper consists of two "banks," occupying the upper and lower halves of the main chart space. These two banks are exactly alike. Each represents a doubling of prices from its bottom to its top, so that whatever value is assigned to the center line, the top line will be twice that figure and the bottom line will be half of it. Let us say the center point is marked 20; then the top will be 40 and the nine intermediate lines will be 22, 24, 26, 28, 30, 32, 34, 36, and 38, reading from center to top, with each of the smallest spaces representing ¼ point. In the lower half of the chart, the bottom line will be 10, the intermediate heavy lines to the center will be 11, 12, 13, 14, 15, 16, 17, 18, and 19, and each of the smallest spaces will be ⅛ point. Because the spaces get smaller as one goes up the chart, one bank shades into the next, making a continuous scale. Clearly, you could have 20 at the top, 10 at the center, and 5 at the bottom; or 10 at the top, 5 at the center, and 2½ at the bottom.

You may have some trouble at first with the different values assigned to the small spaces at different price levels; you may wonder whether a single small space represents ¼ or ⅛ or perhaps a full point. Do not let this bother you. You can see from the scale where 19 is and where 20 is, and obviously 19½ is the midpoint, 19¼ is one-quarter of the way up, and so on. Very quickly, you will find that your mind and your eye adjust almost instantly without any conscious thought or effort.

Where a stock goes off the top or bottom of the paper, it is a simple matter to rescale by moving the chart scale down one bank. If the chart runs off the top at 40, mark the center of the paper 40; the top becomes 80 and the bottom, 20.

For uniformity, and because the paper is so ruled that you can divide either bank of the heavy intermediate lines into 10 parts, with smaller spaces representing standard stock-trading fractions of these main divisions, you must use the figures 5, 10, 20, 40, 80, etc. as the values for the center lines, tops, and bottoms of charts.

For selection of scales on stocks for which you are starting new charts, use the table below.

If the stock now sells between	Center line will be	Top	Bottom
A			
224 and 448	320	640	160
112 and 224	160	320	80
56 and 112	80	160	40
28 and 56	40	80	20
14 and 28	20	40	10
7 and 14	10	20	5
3½ and 7	5	10	2½
1¾ and 3½	2½	5	1¼
a			

(This table can, of course, be continued up or down as far as necessary by multiplying or dividing the key figures by 2.)

The Time Scale

The paper provides for a full year of charting. The sheet is divided into 53 weeks, each consisting of 6 days in which the heavier line represents a Saturday; this is ordinarily left blank because the major markets are not open on Saturday. However, the heavier line will serve to make it easier to locate a day, within a week, quickly. The omission of the Saturday will not perceptibly affect the trend of the technical patterns. Holidays, when they occur, are skipped. Usually a small "H" is inserted at the bottom of the chart to note the holiday and explain the break in the chart. Many technicians start their charts as of the first of a calendar year, filling in the dates of Saturdays, marking the end of each week at the bottom of the paper in the spaces provided, and immediately above these dates, the months.

There is no reason, however, that charts cannot be started at any time, and, if you keep a large number of charts, it may be a help to start some of these in each calendar quarter. Thus, you might start all charts from A to F in January, from G to M in April, from N to S in July, and from T to Z in October.

The Volume Scale

The volume scale that has proved most satisfactory is arithmetic; that is, each unit measured vertically represents the same number of shares traded. Space for volume entries is provided in a special section above the dates. At one time, a logarithmic volume scale was used, but it was given up because the highly significant volumes on very active days tended to be compressed, while low volume in periods of dullness was given too much emphasis. It is necessary to determine the proper figures for the volume scale. No rule for this can be suggested. It is simply a matter of trial and error. With a little experience you will be able to estimate, from your knowledge of the stock you are about to chart, about how much volume is likely to appear on very active days, and you can set up a volume scale that will allow for the maximum expected peak. What you want to avoid is the situation in which volume too frequently runs beyond the top of the volume section; it should do this only at times of unusual activity. When a stock is new to you and you have no knowledge of its habits, it may be best to mark a tentative volume scale, lightly and in pencil, and to keep the volume on this scale for a few weeks. Then, if it is necessary to change the scale, you can do so without having to redraw the entire chart.

Ex-Dividends and Split-Ups

When a stock goes "ex-dividend," "ex-rights," etc., the price will usually drop approximately the amount of the benefit that was "ex." A note should be made on the chart on this day, and it can be entered conveniently at the very bottom, below the dates, showing the amount of the dividend, approximate value of the rights, or other benefits. If the amount involved was substantial and the price drop large enough to require explanation, a dotted line may be drawn vertically on that date from the old price to the "ex" price, showing that this drop was not a market fluctuation but merely the adjustment of price to the distribution.

In the case of a split-up, spin-off, or other capital change, a similar procedure is followed. If the stock is split three shares for one, for example, the price level will change and the chart will be continued at a new level. A dotted vertical line plus an explanatory note will make clear what happened. To get continuity of the chart in such a case, the previous price pattern can be traced and then transferred with carbon paper in the correct position to give a continuous chart adjusted to the new basis for as far back as you need it.

However, if a stock is split two shares for one or four for one, you will not have to make any change in the chart except to note the fact of the split, and to change the scale by dividing all figures by 2 or 4 as the case may be.

In other words, if a stock has been selling at $80 and is split two for one, we simply rescale the chart with the price at $40 and carry on. Often it will help to rule a vertical red line through the date on which a split-up or other capital adjustment takes effect.

Just to reiterate what has been explained previously regarding the mechanical details of charting:

1. Ordinarily, each day's high and low prices are connected by a vertical line, and the last or closing price is indicated by a short horizontal line which may be redrawn toward the right. The open, if used, is drawn to the left. Volume is shown on a special scale at the bottom of the chart, and notes as to ex-dividend dates and amounts of dividends, ex-rights, ex-distributions, split-ups, stock dividends, etc. as they occur may be noted below the volume. Other notes, clippings, record of purchase and sale, and other memos may be written or attached to the chart where they will be conveniently at hand each day.

2. The Tekniplat charting paper is ruled for a 6-day week, although the market operates only from Monday through Friday. The heavy line indicating a Saturday is not used, but, because it provides a little break each week, it makes the plotting of the market days much easier, does not materially affect the accuracy of the chart, nor distort appreciably the trendlines, patterns, etc. Holidays that occur during the business week are simply skipped and left blank,

and the fact that the omitted day was a holiday may be indicated by placing the letter "H" at the bottom of the chart.

The most important factor in charting, of course, is to keep the charts up-to-date. It will pay to take some time to plan how, where, and when to keep one's charts. If possible, find a place, at home or at your office, where you can be relatively free from interference for at least long enough each day to post your charts. Experiment a bit with the placement of desk or table so that you will be getting the best light possible without sharp shadows and without glare. Have binders or folders so that you can keep your charts in a convenient arrangement, easily accessible. Try various grades of pens or pencils to find which will give you the best results. And have a definite place, a drawer or box, where you can keep an adequate supply of pencils, erasers, triangles, ruler, or whatever other equipment you may need.

The most important caution for the beginner who is starting a set of charts for the first time is not to bite off more than he can handle easily! It is a great temptation to set up a large portfolio at the very start. But when some unexpected interruption occurs, such as a day of illness, a trip out of town, or some emergency work, the charts may be neglected for 1 day, 2 days, 3 days, and, with each passing day, the load multiplies. Many enthusiastic beginners have thus become discouraged and have given up the work before they were fairly into it. It is better to take a smaller group than one feels he might want, but which he is sure he can keep up without strain, and then, with increasing speed and greater familiarity with the method, to add stocks gradually as needed.

CHARTING IN THE COMPUTER AGE

Alas! (or as Malraux would have said, *Hélas*!) most of the readers of this book will never know the joys (overrated) of manual charting, just as they will have to consult a dictionary upon reading such terms as "typewriter" and "slide rule." Instead, as all modern readers do, they will have the greatest invention since the quill pen at their fingertips — namely, the personal computer.

The drudgery and tedium (to some) of manual charting has been replaced by the extreme facility of computer-based charting. Numerous (too numerous to enumerate here) software packages are available to assist the moderately competent cyber investor in analyzing the markets. In Appendix D, these resources are detailed. In addition, software is not even necessary if the investor has a connection to the Internet, as there are a multitude of Internet sites which beg to assist the investor in charting, analyzing, dissecting, and trading stocks. These sites are also detailed in Appendix D.

What everyone — the software packages, the Internet sites, the gurus, the talking heads, the wise books, the preternaturally gifted brokerage firms with their precocious pundits — forgot to tell the investor was what is important about this flood of technology.

What Is Important About This Technology

Computer charting and analysis is only a tool. A powerful tool, but just a tool. All the analytical techniques in the world running on the most powerful supercomputers in the world cannot equal experienced and trained judgment in making decisions about stocks. I like to tell the story about the extremely sophisticated (Berkeley Ph.D.s) and educated group I know which, at an enormous expenditure of time and money, created a system that was nearly perfect in trading the markets. Its only problem was it was so complex that it could not be run in market real-time.

It is true that in the area of quantitative analysis, the application of these tools has resulted in noticeable success — particularly among market makers such as Hull Trading Co. and Chicago Research and Trading Co. of the Chicago Board of Options Exchange. The novice should be informed, though, that this success is only partially due to technology. The options markets are amenable to model-based trading, unlike stock and commodity markets. This is because they are based on models — such as the Black-Scholes options pricing model. The stock markets are behavioral markets. Also, market makers have several built-in "edges," the most important of them being the bid–ask spread.

Thus computer tools are really only a brute advance over Tekniplat charting paper, ruler, and pencil and may have the disadvantage of depriving the trader of "feel" that comes with hard work. On the other hand, this brute advance allows the investor to process — or filter — an unlimited number of stocks. Filtering simply means establishing some criteria as to stocks that will be considered. For example, we might say that we wanted only to look at stocks above their 150-day moving average, or above their 4-week high. That would be a filter. And it could be applied literally to *all* stocks.

This ability to process large numbers of stocks — as it were to maintain an enormous chart case — can be important if the investor is running an MEI, in which case it would be necessary to look at and classify the chart of each issue in the group under study.

In addition, experimentation and play with the data are unrestricted. The investor can skip merrily from daily to weekly to monthly, from bar charts to candlestick to point-and-figure, ad infinitum.

In the end, the ability to accomplish and compress this large amount of effort with this tool is the most important element of computer analysis.

Further investigation of computer software and technology, including references to Internet sites, may be pursued in Appendix D.

At the turn of the millennium, the Exchanges are finally switching their systems to trade stocks in pennies instead of fractions — reluctantly. So soon the old Tekniplat chart paper will, like the slide rule, be obsolete. At the Web site (www.johnmageeta.com) investors interested in manual charting will be able to get chart paper designed for the new market facts — decimals and 24/7 trading.

Appendix C

CONTINUING STUDY PLAN

On further study of chart-based technical analysis:

Edwards, Robert D., Magee, John, and Bassetti, W. H. C., *Technical Analysis of Stock Trends*, 8th ed., Boca Raton, FL: St. Lucie Press, 2001.

(This original and definitive work in the field also covers numerous subjects that will be of interest to readers of this book: Pragmatic Portfolio Theory, risk measurement and control, and related topics.)

On credited graduate study seminars open to the public:

Golden Gate University, www.ggu.edu, cdilosa@ggu.edu.
John Magee Web site, www.johnmageeta.com

On volatilities and options:

(and futures)	www.cboe.com
DOW futures and options	www.cbot.com
AMEX ishares (DIA, QQQ, SPY)	www.amex.com

McMillan, Lawrence G., *Options as a Strategic Investment*, New York: New York Institute of Finance, 1993, www.optionstrategist.com

On risk:

Bernstein, Peter, *Against the Gods*, New York: John Wiley & Sons, 1996.
Jorion, Philippe, *Value at Risk*, New York: John Wiley & Sons, 1996.
Risk Management 101 (software), Zoologic Inc., New York.
Edwards, Magee, Bassetti, *Technical Analysis of Stock Trends,* 8th ed., St. Lucie Press, Boca Raton, FL, 2001.

On candlesticks:

Nison, Steve, *Japanese Candlestick Charting Techniques*, New York: New York Institute of Finance, 1991.
Nison, Steve, *Beyond Candlesticks*, New York: John Wiley & Sons, 1994.

On point-and-figure charting:

Cohen, A.W., *How to Use the Three Point Reversal Method of Point and Figure Stock Market Trading*, Larchmont, NY: Chartcraft, 1984.
Bassetti, W. H. C., Bassetti, C. D. H., *Technical Analysis: Natural and Unnatural Methods*, San Geronimo, CA: Maomao Press, 2002.

On developing moving average systems:

See Schwager, below.
DeMark, Thomas, *The New Science of Technical Analysis*, New York: John Wiley & Sons, 1994.

On futures:

Schwager, Jack, *Schwager on Futures, Technical Analysis*, New York: John Wiley & Sons, 1996.

On portfolio management:

The *Journal of Portfolio Management*
Risk Management 101 (software), Zoologic, Inc.

On day trading and short term tactics:

Wyckoff, R. D. and Bassetti, W. H. C., *Technical Analysis for Tacticians*, San Geronimo, CA: Maomao Press, 2002.

Appendix D

RESOURCES

SEC enforcement	enforcement@sec.gov

(Whenever I receive touts or investment spam, I immediately forward it to this important branch of the SEC. All responsible investors should do the same.)

john magee technical analysis::delphic options research ltd (jmta::dor)

email	johnmageeta@johnmageeta.com
jmta::dor website	www.johnmageeta.com
TEKNIPLAT chart paper	visit www.johnmageeta.com
Volatilities and options:	www.optionstrategist.com
	www.cboe.com
Software reviews and info	www.traders.com
Software demos and packages	www.omegaresearch.com
	www.comstar.com
	www.aiq.com
	www.tradestation.com
	www.equis.com
Web analysis site	www.prophetfinance.com
Morningstar	www.morningstar.net

Of General Interest

AARP Investment Program	www.aarp.scudder.com
Accutrade	www.accutrade.com
ADR.com	www.adr.com
American Association of Individual Investors	www.aaii.com

American Century	www.americancentury.com
American Express Financial Services	www.americanexpress.com/direct
(American Express now advertises free trades for some accounts)	
American Stock Exchange	www.amex.com
Ameritrade (has little-advertised site for free trades)	www.ameritrade.com
Annual Report Gallery	www.reportgallery.com
Barron's	www.barrons.com
BigCharts	www.bigcharts.com
Bloomberg Financial	www.bloomberg.com
Bonds Online	www.bondsonline.com
Briefing.com	www.briefing.com
Brill's Mutual Funds Interactive	www.fundsinteractive.com
Business Week	www.businessweek.com
CBS MarketWatch	www.marketwatch.com
Charles Schwab	www.schwab.com
Chicago Board of Options Exchange	www.cboe.com
CNNFN	www.cnnfn.com
DailyStocks	www.dailystocks.com
Excite	www.excite.com
Federal Deposit Insurance Corp	www.fdic.gov
Federal Trade Commission	www.ftc.gov
Fidelity Investments	www.fidelity.com
Financial Times	www.ft.com
Forrester Research	www.forrester.com
FundFocus	www.fundfocus.com
Fund Spot	www.fundspot.com
Gomez Advisers	www.gomez.com
H&R Block	www.hrblock.com
Hoover's StockScreener	www.stockscreener.com
IPO Central	www.ipocentral.com
Lombard	www.lombard.com
Marketplayer	www.marketplayer.com
Market Technician's Assoc.	www.mta.org
Microsoft MoneyCentral	www.moneycentral.com

Morningstar	www.morningstar.net
National Assoc. of Securities Dealers	www.nasd.com
National Discount Brokers	www.ndb.com
Net Investor	www.netinvestor.com
New York Stock Exchange	www.nyse.com
Online Investor	www.onlineinvestor.com
Philadelphia Stock Exchange	www.phlx.com
Quick & Reilly	www.quickwaynet.com
Quicken	www.quicken.com
Quicken Financial Network	www.qfn.com
Realty Stocks	www.realtystocks.com
Reuters	www.reuters.com
SEC Enforcement	enforcement@sec.gov
Securities and Exchange Commission	www.sec.gov
Securities Industry Association	www.sia.com
Securities Investor Protection Corporation	www.sipc.org
SmartMoney	www.smartmoney.com
Social Security Online	www.ssa.gov
Standard & Poor's Fund Analyst	www.micropal.com
Standard & Poor's Ratings Services	www.ratingsdirect.com
Stock Guide	www.stockguide.com
Stockpoint	www.stockpoint.com
Suretrade	www.suretrade.com
1040.com	www.1040.com
The Motley Fool	www.fool.com
TheStreet.com	www.thestreet.com
T. Rowe Price	www.troweprice.com
TreasuryDirect	www.publicdebt.treas.gov
Vanguard Brokerage Services	www.vanguard.com
Wall Street Access	www.wsaccess.com
Wall Street Journal Interactive Ed.	www.wsj.com
Yahoo! Finance	www.quote.yahoo.com
Zacks Investment Research	www.zacks.com
ZD Interactive Investor	www.zdii.com

Brokerage Houses

A. B. Watley	www.abwatley.com	888-229-2853
Accutrade	www.accutrade.com	800-494-8939
Ameritrade	www.ameritrade.com	800-326-7507
Ameritrade (2nd site)	www.freetrade.com	
Charles Schwab	www.schwab.com	800-435-4000
Datek Online	www.datek.com	
Discover Brokerage	www.discoverbrokerage.com	800-688-3462
DLJ Direct	www.dljdirect.com	800-825-5723
Dow-Jones Markets	www.djmarkets.com	
DRIP Central	www.dripcentral.com	
E*TRADE	www.etrade.com	800-786-2575
Empire Financial Group, Inc.	www.lowfees.com	800-900-8101
Jack White	www.jackwhiteco.com	800-753-1700
Lombard	www.lombard.com	
National Discount Brokers	www.ndb.com	800-888-3999
Net Investor	www.netinvestor.com	800-638-4250
Quick & Reilly	www.quickwaynet.com	800-672-7220
Suretrade	www.suretrade.com	401-642-6900
Vanguard Brokerage Services	www.vanguard.com	800-992-8327
Wall Street Access	www.wsaccess.com	888-925-5782
Waterhouse Securities	www.waterhouse.com	800-934-4134
Web Street Securities	www.webstreetsecurities.com	800-932-0438
WitCapital	www.witcapital.com	888-494-8227

GLOSSARY

Accumulation: The first phase of a bull market. The period when far-sighted investors begin to buy shares from discouraged or distressed sellers. Financial reports are usually at their worst and the public is completely disgusted with the stock market. Volume is only moderate but beginning to increase on the rallies.

Activity: *See* Volume.

Apex: The highest point; the pointed end or tip of a triangle.

Arbitrage: The simultaneous buying and selling of two different, but closely related, instruments to take advantage of a disparity in their prices in one market or different markets; for example, the discount of Dow-Jones futures to cash would result in the immediate purchase of futures and the sale of cash. In takeovers or acquisitions this is not arbitrage, but spreading, ersatz arbitrage, or faux arbitrage. True arbitrage has two forms, strong and weak (or risk). Strong arbitrage realizes a profit when initiated and only requires time or distance to realize the profit. Weak or risk arbitrage has uncontrolled factors, or factors that must be constantly adjusted to realize the profit.

Area gap: *See* Common gap.

Area pattern: When a stock or commodity's upward or downward momentum has been temporarily exhausted, the ensuing sideways movement in the price usually traces out a design or arrangement of form called an area pattern. The shape of some of these area patterns, or formations, has predictive value under certain conditions. *See* Ascending triangle, Broadening formations, Descending triangle, Diamond, Flag, Head and shoulders, Inverted triangle, Pennant, Rectangle, Right-angle triangles, Symmetrical triangles, and Wedges.

Arithmetic scale: Price or volume scale where the distance on the vertical axis (i.e., space between horizontal lines) represents equal amounts of dollars or number of shares.

Ascending (parallel) trend channel: When the tops of the rallies composing an advance develop along a line (sometimes called a return line), which is also parallel to the basic up trendline (i.e., the line that

217

slopes up across the wave bottoms in an advance); the area between the two lines is called an ascending or up channel.

Ascending (up) trendline: The advancing wave in a stock or commodity is composed of a series of ripples. When the bottoms of these ripples form on, or very close to, an upward-slanting straight line, a basic ascending or up trendline is formed.

Ascending triangle: One of a class of area patterns called right-angle triangles. The class is distinguished by the fact that one of the two boundary lines is practically horizontal while the other slants toward it. If the top line is horizontal, and the lower slants upward to an intersection point to the right, the resulting area pattern is called an ascending triangle. The implication is bullish, with the expectant breakout though the horizontal line. Measuring formula: add the broadest part of triangle to the breakout point.

At the money: An option, the strike price of which is equal to the market value of the underlying futures contract or instrument.

Averages: *See* Dow-Jones Industrial Averages, Moving averages, Dow-Jones Transportation Averages, and Dow-Jones Utility Averages.

Averaging cost: An investing technique in which the investor buys a stock or commodity at successively lower prices, thereby "averaging down" his average cost of each stock share or commodity contract. Purchases at successively higher prices would "average up" the price of stock shares or commodity contracts. It is an invention of the financial industry to bamboozle an investor uninformed enough to practice this shuffle.

Axis: In the graphical sense, an axis is a straight line for measurement or reference. It is also the line, real or imagined, on which a formation is regarded as rotating.

Balanced program: Proportioning capital, or a certain part of capital, equally between the long side and the short side of the market, and or amongst different asset classes.

Bar chart: Also called a line or vertical chart. A graphic representation of prices using a vertical bar to connect the highest price in the time period to the lowest price. Opening prices are noted with a small horizontal line to the left. Closing prices are shown with a small horizontal line to the right. Bar charts can be constructed for any time period in which prices are available. The most common time periods found in bar charts are hourly, daily, weekly, and monthly. However, with the growing number of personal computers and the availability of "real-time" quotes, it is not unusual for traders to use some period of minutes to construct a bar chart.

Basing point: The price level in the chart that determines where a stop loss point is placed. As technical conditions change, the basing point, and stops, can be advanced (in a rising market) or lowered (in a falling market). *See* Progressive stops.

Basic trendlines: *See* Trendlines.

Basis points: The measure of yields on bonds and notes; one basis point equals 0.01% of yield.

Basket trades: Large transactions made up of a number of various stocks.

Bear market: In its simplest form, a bear market is a period when prices are primarily declining, usually for a long period. Bear markets generally consist of three phases: the first phase is distribution; the second is panic; the third is akin to a washout, where those investors who have held out through the first two phases finally give up and liquidate.

Bent neckline: *See* Neckline.

Beta: A measure of sensitivity to market swings.

Beta (coefficient): A measure of the market or nondiversifiable risk associated with any given security in the market.

Block trades: Large transactions of a particular stock sold as a unit.

Blow-off: *See* Climactic top.

Blue chips: The nickname given to generally high-priced companies with good records of earnings, dividends, and price stability. Also called gilt-edged securities. Examples are IBM, AT&T, General Motors and General Electric.

Book value: The theoretical measure of what a stock is worth based on the value of the company's assets less the company's debt.

Bottom: *See* Ascending triangle, Dormant bottom, Double bottom, Head-and-shoulders (Kilroy) bottom, Rounding bottom, and Selling climax.

Boundary: The edges of a pattern.

Bowl: *See* Rounding bottom.

Bracketing: A trading range market or a price area that is nontrending.

Breakaway gap: The hole or gap in the chart created when a stock or commodity breaks out of an area pattern.

Breakout: When a stock or commodity exits an area pattern.

Broadening formation: Sometimes called inverted triangles, these are formations that start with narrow fluctuations that widen between diverging, rather than converging, boundary lines. *See also* Right-angled broadening triangle, Broadening formation, Broadening top, Head-and-shoulders top, and Diamond patterns.

Broadening top: An area reversal pattern that may evolve in any one of three forms, comparable in shape, respectively, to inverted symmetrical, ascending, or descending triangles. Unlike triangles, however, the tops and bottoms of these patterns do not necessarily stop at clearly marked diverging boundary lines. Volume, rather than diminishing in triangles, tends to be unusually high and irregular throughout pattern construction. No measuring formula is available.

Bull market: A period when prices are primarily rising, normally for an extended period. Usually, but not always, divisible into three phases. The first phase is accumulation. The second phase is one of fairly steady advance with increasing volume. And the third phase is marked by considerable activity as the public begins to recognize and attempt to profit from the rising market.

Call: An option that gives the buyer the right to buy the underlying instrument at a specific price within a certain time period and which obligates the seller to sell the instrument.

Call margin: *See* Margin call.

Candlestick chart: Japanese charting method where bars are color coded according to direction of price movement.

Cats and dogs: Low-priced stocks of questionable investment value.

Channel: If the tops of the rallies and bottoms of the reactions develop lines that are approximately parallel to one another, the area between these lines is called a channel. *See also* Ascending trend channel, Descending trend channel, and Horizontal trend channel.

Chart: A graphic representation of a stock or commodity in terms of price and or volume. *See also* Bar chart, Candlestick chart, and Point-and-figure chart.

Clean-out day: *See* Selling climax.

Climactic top: A sharp advance, accompanied by extraordinary volume (i.e., much larger volume than the normal increase), which signals the final "blow-off" of the trend, followed by either a reversal or at least by a period of stagnation, formation of consolidation pattern, or a correction.

Climax day: *See* One-day reversal.

Climax, selling: *See* Selling climax.

Closing price: The last sale price of the trading session for a stock. In commodities it represents an official price determined from a range of prices deemed to have traded at or on the close; also called a settlement price.

Closing the gap: When a stock or commodity returns to a previous gap and retraces the range of the gap. Also called "covering the gap" or "filling the gap." *See* Gap.

Coil: Another term for a symmetrical triangle.

Commission: The amount charged by a brokerage house to execute a trade in a stock, option, or commodity transaction. A commission is charged for each purchase and each sale. In commodities, a commission is charged only when the original entry trade has been closed with an offsetting trade. This is called a round-turn commission.

Common gap: Also called area gap. Any hole or gap in the chart occurring within an "area pattern." The forecasting significance of the common gap is nil. *See* Gap.

Comparative relative strength: Compares the price movement of a stock with that of its competitors, industry group, or the whole market.

Complex head-and-shoulders: Also called "multiple head and shoulders," it is a head-and-shoulders pattern with more than one right and left shoulder and or head. *See* Head-and-shoulders pattern.

Composite average: A stock average composed of the 65 stocks that make up the Dow-Jones industrial average and the Dow-Jones utility average.

Composite leverage: In the Edwards and Magee book, *Technical Analysis of Stock Trends*, it is a formula for combining the principal factors affecting a given sum of capital used (i.e., sensitivity, price, and margin) into one index figure.

Confirmation: In a pattern, it is the point at which a stock or commodity exits an area pattern in the expected direction by an amount of price and volume sufficient to meet minimum pattern requirements for a bona fide breakout. In the Dow Theory, it means both the industrial average and the transportation average have registered new highs or lows during the same advance or decline. If only one of the averages establishes a new high (or low) and the other one does not, it would be a nonconfirmation, or divergence. This is also true of oscillators. To confirm a new high (or low) in a stock or commodity an oscillator needs to reach a new high (or low) as well. Failure of the oscillator to confirm a new high (or low) is called a divergence and would be considered an early indication of a potential reversal in direction.

Congestion: The sideways trading from which area patterns evolve. Not all congestion periods produce a recognizable pattern, however.

Consolidation pattern: Also called a continuation pattern, it is an area pattern which breaks out in the direction of the previous trend. *See* Ascending triangle, Descending triangle, Flag, Head-and-shoulders consolidation, Pennant, Rectangle, Scallop, and Symmetrical triangle.

Continuation gap: *See* Runaway gap.

Continuation pattern: *See* Consolidation pattern.

Convergent pattern (trend): Those patterns with upper and lower boundary lines that meet, or converge, at some point if extended to the right. *See* Ascending triangle, Descending triangle, Symmetrical triangle, Wedges, and Pennants.

Correction: A move in a commodity or stock that is opposite to the prevailing trend but not sufficient to change that trend; called a rally in a downtrend and a reaction in an uptrend. In the Dow Theory, a correction is a secondary trend against the primary trend, that usually lasts from 3 weeks to 3 months and retraces from one-third to two-thirds of the preceding swing in the primary direction.

Covering the gap: *See* Closing the gap.

Cradle: The intersection of the two converging boundary lines of a symmetrical triangle. *See* Apex.

Daily range: The difference between the high and low price during one trading day.

Demand: Buying interest for a stock at a given price.

Descending (parallel) trend channel: When the bottoms of the reactions comprising a decline develop along a line (sometimes called a return line), that is also parallel to the basic down trendlines (i.e., the line that slopes down across the wave tops in a decline); the area between the two lines is called a descending or down channel.

Descending trendline: The declining wave in a stock or commodity is composed of a series of ripples. When the tops of these ripples form on, or very close to, a downward-slanting straight line, a basic descending or downtrend line is formed.

Descending triangle: One of a class of area patterns called right-angled triangles. The class is distinguished by the fact that one of the two boundary lines is practically horizontal while the other slants toward it. If the bottom line is horizontal and the upper slants downward to an intersection point to the right, the resulting area pattern is called a descending triangle. The implication is bearish, with the expectant breakout through the flat (horizontal) side. Minimum` measuring formula: add the broadest part of the triangle to the breakout point.

Diamond: Usually a reversal pattern, but it will also be found as a continuation pattern. It could be described as a complex head-and-shoulders pattern with a V-shaped (bent) neckline, or a broadening pattern that, after two or three swings, changes into a regular triangle. The overall shape is a four-point diamond. Because it requires a fairly active market, it is more often found at major tops. Many complex head-and-shoulder tops are borderline diamond patterns. The major difference is in the right side of the pattern. It should clearly show two converging lines with diminishing volume as in a symmetrical triangle. Minimum measuring formula: add the greatest width of the pattern to the breakout point.

Distribution: The first phase of a bear market which really begins in the last stage of a bull market. The period when far-sighted investors sense that the market has outrun its fundamentals and begin to unload their holdings at an increasing pace. Trading volume is still high; however, it tends to diminish on rallies. The public is still active but beginning to show signs of caution as hoped-for profits fade away.

Divergence: When new highs (or lows) in one indicator are not realized in another comparable indicator. *See* Confirmation.

Divergent pattern (trend): Those patterns with upper and lower boundary lines that meet at some point if extended to the left. *See* Broadening formation.

Diversification: The concept of placing one's funds in different industry groups and investment vehicles to spread risk. Not placing all one's financial eggs in one basket.

Dividends: A share of the profits — in cash or stock equivalent — that is paid to stockholders.

Dormant bottom: A variation of a rounding (bowl) bottom, but in an extended, flat-bottomed form. It usually appears in "thin" stocks (i.e., those issues with a small number of shares outstanding) and, characteristically, will show lengthy periods during which no sales will be registered for days at a time. The chart will appear "fly-specked" due to the missing days. The technical implication is for an upside breakout.

Double bottom: Reversal pattern. A bottom formed on relatively high volume that is followed by a rally (of at least 15%) and then a second bottom (possibly rounded) at the same level (plus or minus 3%) as the first bottom on lower volume. A rally back though the apex of the intervening rally confirms the reversal. More than a month should separate the two bottoms. Minimum measuring formula: Take the distance from the lowest bottom to the apex of the intervening rally and add it to the apex.

Double top: A high-volume top is formed followed by a reaction (of at least 15%) on diminishing activity. Another rally back to the previous high (plus or minus 3%) is made, but on lower volume than the first high. A decline through the low of the reaction confirms the reversal. The two highs should be more than a month apart. Minimum measuring formula: Add to the breakout point the distance from the highest peak to the low of the reaction. Also called an "M" formation.

Double trendline: When two relatively close parallel trendlines are needed to define the true trend pattern. *See* Trendline.

Dow-Jones Industrial Average: Developed by Charles Dow in 1885 to study market trends. Originally composed of 14 companies (12 railroads and 2 industrials), the rails by 1897 were separated into their own average, and 12 industrial companies of the day were selected for the industrial average. The number was increased to 20 in 1916 and to 30 in 1928. The stocks included in this average have been changed from time to time to keep the list up to date, or to accommodate a merger. The only original issue still in the average is General Electric.

Dow-Jones Transportation Average: Established at the turn of the century with the new industrial average, it was originally called the Rails Average and was composed of 20 railroad companies. With the advent of the airlines industry the average was updated in 1970 and the name changed to Transportation Average.

Dow-Jones Utility Average: In 1929, utility companies were dropped from the Industrial Average and a new utility average of 20 companies was created. In 1938, the number of issues was reduced to the present 15.

Downtick: A securities transaction that is at a price that is lower than the preceding transaction;

Downtrend: *See* Descending trendline and Trend.

End run: When a breakout of a symmetrical triangle pattern reverses its direction and trades back through support (if an upside breakout) or resistance (if a downside breakout), it is termed an "end run around the line," or "end run" for short. The term is sometimes used to denote breakout failure in general.

Equilibrium market: A price area that represents a balance between demand and supply.

Ex-dividend: The day when the dividend is subtracted from the price of the stock.

Ex-dividend gap: The gap in price caused when the price of a stock is adjusted downward after the dividend payment is deducted.

Exercise: The means by which the holder of an option purchases or sells shares of the underlying security.

Exhaustion gap: Relatively wide gap in the price of a stock or commodity that occurs near the end of a strong directional move in the price. These gaps are quickly closed, most often within 2 to 5 days, which helps to distinguish them from runaway gaps which are not usually covered for a considerable length of time. An exhaustion gap cannot be read as a major reversal, or even necessarily a reversal. It signals a halt in the prevailing trend which is ordinarily followed by some sort of area pattern development.

Expiration: The last day on which an option can be exercised.

Exponential smoothing: A mathematical-statistical methodology of forecasting that assumes future price action is a weighted average of past periods; a mathematical series in which greater weight is given to more recent price action.

Falling wedge: An area pattern with two downward-slanting, converging trendlines. Normally it takes more than 3 weeks to complete, and volume will diminish as prices move toward the apex of the pattern. The anticipated direction of the breakout in a falling wedge is up. Minimum measuring formula: A retracement of all the ground lost within the wedge. *See* Wedge.

False breakout: A breakout that is confirmed but that quickly reverses and eventually leads the stock or commodity to a breakout in the opposite direction. Indistinguishable from premature breakout or genuine breakout when it occurs.

Fan lines: A set of three secondary trendlines drawn from the same starting high or low, that spread out in a fan shape. In a primary uptrend, the fan would be along the tops of the secondary (intermediate) reaction. In a primary downtrend, the fan would be along the bottoms of the secondary (intermediate) rally. When the third fan line is broken, it signals the resumption of the primary trend.

50-day moving-average line: Determined by summing the closing price over the past 50 trading days and dividing by 50, and so on.

Five-point reversal: *See* Broadening pattern.

Flag continuation pattern: A flag is a period of congestion, less than 4 weeks in duration, that forms after a sharp, near vertical, change in price. The upper and lower boundary lines of the pattern are parallel, though both may slant up, down, or sideways. In an uptrend, the pattern resembles a flag flying from a mast, hence the name. Flags are also called measuring or half-mast patterns because they tend to form at the midpoint of the rally or reaction. Volume tends to diminish during the formation and increase on the breakout. Minimum measuring formula: add the distance from the breakout point, which started the preceding "mast" rally or reaction, to the breakout point of the flag.

Floating supply: The number of shares available for trading at any given time. Generally the outstanding number of shares, less shares closely held and likely to be unavailable to the public. Shares of a company held by its employee pension fund, for example, would not generally enter the trading stream and could be subtracted from the outstanding shares.

Formation: *See* Area patterns.

Front-month: The first expiration month in a series of months.

Fundamental: Information on a stock pertaining to the business of the company and how it relates to earnings and dividends. In a commodity, it would be information on any factor that would affect supply or demand.

Futures: An investment contract between buyer and seller in which the parties contract to receive or deliver the underlying instrument at a fixed price by a fixed time in the future. Generally a speculative instrument that requires very low "margins" (or performance bonds) but that is marked to market daily, requiring the losing party to supply cash as his equity fluctuates. Used extensively for hedging by commercials — grain companies, mining companies, etc. Primary importance to stock traders are futures contracts on the Industrials and the S&P at the CBOT.

Gap: A hole in the price range that occurs when either (1) the lowest price at which a stock or commodity is traded during any time period is higher than the highest price at which it was traded on the preceding time period, or (2) the highest price of one time period is lower than the lowest price of the preceding time period. When the ranges of the two time periods are plotted, they will not overlap or touch the same horizontal level on the chart — there will be a price gap between them. *See* Common or Area gap, Ex-dividend gap, Breakaway gap, Runaway gap, Exhaustion gap, and Island reversal.

Graph: *See* Chart.

Half-mast formation: *See* Flag continuation pattern.

Head-and-shoulders pattern: In its normal form, this pattern is one of the more common and more reliable of the major reversal patterns. It consists of the following four elements (a head and shoulders top will be described for illustration): (1) a rally which ends a more or less extensive advance on heavy volume, and which is then followed by a minor reaction on less volume — this is the left shoulder; (2) another high-volume advance which exceeds the high of the left shoulder, followed by another low-volume reaction which takes prices down to near the bottom of the preceding reaction, and below the top of the left shoulder high — this is the head; (3) a third rally, but on decidedly less volume than accompanied either of the first two advances, and which fails to exceed the high established on the head — this is the right shoulder; and (4) a decline through a line drawn across the preceding two reaction lows (the neckline), and a close below that line equivalent to 3% of the stock's market price — this is the confirmation of the breakout. A head-and-shoulders or Kilroy bottom, or any other combination head-and-shoulders pattern, contains the same four elements inverted. The main difference between a top formation and a bottom formation is in the volume patterns. The breakout in a top can be on low volume. The breakout in a bottom must show a "conspicuous burst of activity." Minimum measuring formula: add the distance between the head and neckline to the breakout point. Occasionally an inverted head-and-shoulders or Kilroy pattern (called a consolidation head-and-shoulders) will form which is a continuation pattern.

Head-and-shoulders bottom: Area pattern that reverses a decline. *See* Head-and-shoulders pattern. Also called Kilroy bottom.

Head-and-shoulders or Kilroy consolidation: Area pattern that continues the previous trend. *See* Head-and-shoulders pattern.

Head-and-shoulders top: Area pattern that reverses an advance. *See* Head-and-shoulders pattern.

Heavy volume: The expression "heavy volume," as used by Edwards and Magee, means heavy only with respect to the recent volume of sales in the stock one is watching.

Hedging: To try to lessen risk by making a counterbalancing investment. In a stock portfolio, an example of a hedge would be to buy 100 shares of XYZ stock, and to buy one put option of the same stock. The put would help protect against a decline in the stock, but it would also limit potential gains on the upside.

Historical data: A series of past daily, weekly, or monthly market prices.

Hook day: A trading day in which the open is above or below prior day's high or low and the close is below or above prior day's close with narrow range.

Horizontal channel: When the tops of the rallies and bottoms of the reactions form along lines that are horizontal and parallel to one another; the area between is called a horizontal trend channel. It may also be called a rectangle during the early stages of formation.

Horizontal trendline: A horizontal line drawn across either the tops or bottoms in a sideways trending market.

Hybrid head-and-shoulders: A small head-and-shoulders pattern within a larger head-and-shoulders pattern. *See* Head-and-shoulders pattern.

Industrial average: *See* Dow-Jones Industrial Average.

Inside day: A day in which the daily price range is totally within the prior day's daily price range.

Insiders: Individuals who possess fundamental information that is likely to affect the price of a stock but which is unavailable to the public. An example would be an individual who knows about a merger before it is announced to the public. Trading by insiders on this type of information is illegal.

Intermediate trend: In the Edwards and Magee book, *Technical Analysis of Stock Trends*, the term "intermediate" or "secondary" refers to a trend (or pattern indicating a trend) against the primary (major) trend that is likely to last from 3 weeks to 3 months, and that may retrace one-third to two-thirds of the previous primary advance or decline.

Inverted bowl: *See* Rounding top.

Inverted triangle: *See* Right-angled broadening triangle.

ishares: Ishares are stock-like instruments (ETF's or Exchange Traded Funds) traded on the American Stock Exchange which represent a small percentage of a major index, for example, the DIA is 10% of the Dow Jones Industrials. See www.amex.com.

Island reversal: A compact trading range, usually formed after a fast rally or reaction, that is separated from the previous move by an exhaustion gap, and from the move in the opposite direction that follows by a breakaway gap. The result is an island of prices detached by a gap before and after. If the trading range contains only 1 day, it is called a 1-day reversal. The two gaps usually occur at approximately the same level. By itself, the pattern is not of major significance, but it does frequently send prices back for a complete retracement of the minor move that preceded it.

Kilroy bottom: See Head-and-shoulders bottom.

Leverage: Using a smaller amount of capital to control an investment of greater value. For example, exclusive of interest and commission costs, if you buy a stock on 50% margin, you control $1 of stock for every 50 cents invested or leverage of 2-to-1.

Limit move: A change in price that exceeds the limits set by the exchange on which the contract or security is traded.

Limit order: A buy or sell order that is limited in some way, usually in price. For example, if you placed a limit order to buy IBM at 100, the broker would not fill the order unless he could do so at your price or better (i.e., at 100 or lower).

Limit up, limit down: Commodity exchange restrictions on the maximum upward or downward movement permitted in the price for a commodity during any trading session.

Line, Dow Theory: A line in the Dow Theory is an intermediate sideways movement in one or both of the averages (industrial and or transportation) in the course of which prices fluctuate within a range of 5% (of mean price) or less.

Logarithmic scale: *See* Semi-logarithmic scale.

Magee Evaluative Index: Constructed by examining each stock in the universe under consideration and ranking it weak, neutral, or strong and compiling the percentages. Extreme readings in the industrials (5–8% strong for bottoms, 80% for tops) mark major market bottoms, and tops.

Major trend: In the Edwards and Magee book, *Technical Analysis of Stock Trends*, the term "major" (or "primary") refers to a trend (or pattern leading to such a trend) that lasts at least 1 year and shows a rise or decline of at least 20%.

Margin: The minimum amount of capital required to buy or sell a stock. The rate, currently 50% of value, is set by the government. In a commodity, margin is also the minimum (usually about 10%) needed to buy or sell a contract. But the rate is set by the individual exchanges. The two differ in cost as well. In a stock, the broker lends the investor the balance of the money due and charges interest for the loan. In a commodity, margin is treated as a good faith payment. The broker does not lend the difference so no interest expense is incurred.

Market on close: An order specification that requires the broker to get the best price available on the close of trading.

Market order: An instruction to buy or sell at the price prevailing when the order reaches the floor of the Exchange.

Market reciprocal: Normal average range of a stock based on the average range for a number of years, divided by the current average range. The result is the reciprocal of the market movement for the period. Wide market activity, for example, would show a small decimal, less than 1. Dull trading would be a larger number.

Mast: The vertical rally or reaction preceding a flag or pennant formation.

Measuring formula: The formula for determining the minimum amount a stock or commodity is likely to move after a successful breakout of an area pattern. See individual patterns for specific formulas.

Measuring gap: *See* Runaway gap.

Minor trend: In the Edwards and Magee book, *Technical Analysis of Stock Trends*, the term "minor" refers to brief fluctuations (usually less than 6 days and rarely longer than 3 weeks) that, in total, make up the intermediate trend.

Momentum indicator: A market indicator that uses volume statistics for predicting the strength or weakness of a current market and any overbought or oversold conditions, and to distinguish turning points within the market.

Money management rules: Per Pragmatic Portfolio Theory, a Portfolio Risk Profile dictates (e.g., how much capital should be risked on any one trade, in any one position, and for the portfolio as a whole). *See* Pragmatic Portfolio Theory. Refer to *Technical Analysis of Stock Trends* (8th ed.).

Moving average: A mathematical technique to smooth data. It is called "moving" because the number of elements are fixed but the time interval advances. Old data must be removed when new data are added, which causes the average to "move along" with the progression of the stock or commodity price.

Moving average crossovers: The point at which the various moving average lines pass through or over each other.

Multiple head-and-shoulders pattern: *See* Complex head-and-shoulders.

Natural systems: Systems based on market data alone without any intervening numerical processes (e.g., chart analysis and high-low systems, as Donchian's systems).

Narrow range day: A trading day with a narrower price range relative to the previous day's price range.

Neckline: In a head-and-shoulders pattern, it is the line drawn across the two reaction lows (in a top), or two rally highs (in a bottom), that occur before and after the head. This line must be broken by 3% to confirm the reversal. In a diamond pattern, which is similar to a head-and-shoulders pattern, the neckline is bent in the shape of a V or inverted V. *See* Diamond pattern and Head-and-shoulders pattern.

Negative divergence: When two or more averages, indices, or indicators fail to show confirming trends.

Odd lot: A block of stock consisting of less than 100 shares.

Operational risk: Determined by taking stop price from market price, in simplest form. For complete exposition refer to *Technical Analysis of Stock Trends* (8th ed.).

One-day reversal: *See* Island reversal.

Option: The right granted to one investor by another to buy (called a call option) or sell (called a put option) 100 shares of stock, or one contract of a commodity, at a fixed price for a fixed period. The investor granting the right (the seller of the option) is paid a nonrefundable premium by the buyer of the option.

Order: *See* Limit order, Market order, and Stop order.

Oscillator: A form of momentum or rate-of-change indicator that is usually valued from +1 to −1 or from 0% to 100%.

Overbought: Market prices that have risen too steeply and too quickly.

Oversold: Market prices that have declined too steeply and too quickly.

Overbought/oversold indicator: An indicator that attempts to define when prices have moved too far and too quickly in either direction and thus are liable to a reaction.

Panic: The second stage of a bear market when buyers thin out and sellers become more urgent. The downward trend of prices suddenly accelerates into an almost vertical drop while volume rises to climactic proportions. *See* Bear market.

Panic bottom: *See* Selling climax.

Pattern: *See* Area pattern.

Peak: *See* Top.

Penetration: The breaking of a pattern boundary line, trendline, or support and resistance level.

Pennant: A pennant is a flag with converging, rather than parallel, boundary lines. *See* Flag continuation pattern.

Point-and-figure chart: A method of charting believed to have been created by Charles Dow. Each day the price moves by a specific amount (the arbitrary box size), an X (if up) or O (if down) is placed on a vertical column of squared paper. As long as prices do not change direction by a specified amount (the reversal), the trend is considered to be in force and no new column is made. If a reversal takes place, another vertical column is started immediately to the right of the first but in the opposite direction. There is no provision for time on a point-and-figure chart.

Portfolio risk: Measured by operational, temporal, and catastrophic elements, reducible to a daily (or any other time frame) figure which may be used to simulate catastrophic risk by assuming x standard deviation moves. Refer to *Technical Analysis of Stock Trends* (8th ed.).

Pragmatic Portfolio Theory: PPT dictates the following: (1) portfolio should be balanced according to the MEI; (2) a continual process of rebalancing occurs, per rhythmic trading; (3) all positions should be risk balanced insofar as possible; (4) that risk measurement is constant in three dimensions: operational, time, catastrophic. For a complete exposition, refer to *Technical Analysis of Stock Trends* (8th ed.).

Premature breakout: A breakout of an area pattern, then a retreat back into the pattern. Eventually the trend will break out again and proceed in the same direction. At the time they occur, false breakouts and premature breakouts are indistinguishable from each other or from a genuine breakout.

Primary trend: *See* Major trend.

Program trading: Trades based on signals from various computer programs, usually entered directly from the trader's computer to the market's computer system. Also futures/cash arbitrage or hedging. Also large transactions of baskets of stock by large traders.

Progressive stop: A stop order that follows the market up or down. *See* Stop.

Protective stop: A stop order used to protect gains or limit losses in an existing position. *See* Stop.

Pullback: Return of prices to the boundary line of the pattern after a breakout to the downside. Return after an upside breakout is called a "throwback."

Put: An option to sell a specified amount of a stock or commodity at an agreed time at the stated exercise price.

Rail Average: *See* Dow-Jones Transportation Average.

Rally: An increase in price that retraces part of the previous price decline.

Rally tops: A price level that finishes a short-term rally in an ongoing trend.

Range: The difference between the high and low during a specific time period.

Reaction: A decline in price that retraces part of the previous price advance.

Reciprocal, market: *See* Market reciprocal.

Recovery: *See* Rally.

Rectangle: A trading area that is bounded on the top and the bottom with horizontal, or near horizontal, lines. A rectangle can be either a reversal or continuation pattern depending on the direction of the breakout. Minimum measuring formula: add the width (difference between top and bottom) of the rectangle to the breakout point.

Resistance level: A price level at which a sufficient supply of stock is forthcoming to stop, and possibly turn back for a time, an uptrend.

Retracement: A price movement in the opposite direction of the previous trend.

Return line: *See* Ascending or Descending trend channels.

Reversal gap: A chart formation where the low of the last day is above the previous day's range with the close above mid-range and above the open.

Reversal pattern: An area pattern that breaks out in a direction opposite to the previous trend. *See* Ascending triangle, Broadening formation, Broadening top, Descending triangle, Diamond, Dormant bottom,

Double bottom or top, Triple bottom or top, Head-and-shoulders, Rectangle, Rounding bottom or top, Saucer, Symmetrical triangle, and Rising or Falling wedge.

Right-angled broadening triangle: Area pattern with one boundary line horizontal and the other at an angle that, when extended, will converge with the horizontal line at some point to the left of the pattern. Similar in shape to ascending and descending triangles except they are inverted and look like flat-topped or bottomed megaphones. Right-angled broadening formations generally carry bearish implications regardless of which side is flat. But any decisive breakout (3% or more) through the horizontal boundary line has the same forceful significance as does a breakout in an ascending or descending triangle.

Right-angled triangles: *See* Ascending and Descending triangles.

Rising wedge: An area pattern with two upward-slanting, converging trendlines. Normally it takes more than 3 weeks to complete, and volume will diminish as prices move toward the apex of the pattern. The anticipated direction of the breakout in a rising wedge is down. Minimum measuring formula: a retracement of all the ground gained within the wedge.

Risk: The variable which must be controlled. In its simplest form the distance between the market price and the stop price on the position. Generally defined as volatility by theorists and academicians.

Risk per trade: RPT is determined by multiplying the position size by the difference between the stop price and the market price. This is constrained by the percentage of capital risk that may be ventured on any one position, such as 3% of capital may be risked on one trade so the position size must be adjusted to fit this constraint. Refer to *Technical Analysis of Stock Trends* (8th ed.).

Round lot: A block of stock consisting of 100 shares of stock.

Round trip: The cost of one complete stock or commodity transaction (i.e., the entry cost and the offset cost combined).

Rounding bottom: An area pattern that pictures a gradual, progressive, and fairly symmetrical change in the trend from down to up. Both the price pattern (along its lows) and the volume pattern show a concave shape, often called a bowl or saucer. There is no minimum measuring formula associated with this reversal pattern.

Rounding top: An area pattern that pictures a gradual, progressive, and fairly symmetrical change in the trend from up to down. The price pattern, along its highs, shows a convex shape sometimes called an inverted bowl. The volume pattern is concave-shaped (a bowl) as trading activity declines into the peak of the price pattern and increases when prices begin to fall. There is no measuring formula associated with this reversal pattern.

Runaway day: A day's trading that traverses a noticeably longer range in one direction than the days around it.

Runaway gap: A relatively wide gap in prices that occurs in an advance or decline gathering momentum. Also called a "measuring gap" as it frequently occurs at just about the halfway point between the breakout that started the move and the reversal day that calls an end to it. Minimum measuring formula: take the distance from the original breakout point to the start of the gap, and add it to the other side of the gap.

Running market: A market wherein prices are moving rapidly in one direction with very few or no price changes in the opposite direction.

Saucer: *See* Rounding bottom and Scallops.

Scallops: A series of rounding bottom (saucers) patterns where the rising end always carries prices a little higher than the preceding top at the beginning of the pattern. Net gains will vary from stock to stock, but there is a strong tendency for it to amount to 10 to 15% of the price. The total reaction, from the lefthand top of each saucer to its bottom, is usually in the 20 to 30% area. Individual saucers in a scallop series are normally 5 to 7 weeks long and rarely less than 3 weeks. The volume will show a convex or bowl pattern.

Secondary trend: *See* Intermediate trend.

Selling climax: A period of extraordinary volume that comes at the end of a rapid and comprehensive decline that exhausts the margin reserves of many speculators and patience of investors. Total volume turnover may exceed any single day's volume during the previous upswing as panic selling sweeps through the stock or commodity. Also called a clean-out day, a selling climax reverses the technical conditions of the market. Although it is a form of a 1-day reversal, it can take more than 1 day to complete.

Semi-logarithmic scale: Price or volume scale on which the distance on the vertical axis (i.e., space between horizontal lines) represents equal percentage changes.

Sensitivity: An index used by Edwards and Magee to measure the probable percentage movement (sensitivity) of a stock during a specified percentage move in the stock market as a whole. Very like beta.

Shake-out: A corrective move large enough to "shake out" nervous investors before the primary trend resumes.

Short interest: The number of shares that have been sold short and not yet repurchased. This information is published monthly by the New York Stock Exchange.

Short sale: A transaction in which the entry position is to sell a stock or commodity first and to repurchase it (hopefully at a lower price) at a later date. In the stock market, shares not owned can be sold by borrowing shares from the broker and replacing them when the offsetting repurchase takes place. In the commodity market, contracts are created when a buyer and seller get together through a floor broker. As a result, the procedure to sell in the commodity market is the same as it is to buy.

Shoulder: *See* Head-and-shoulders patterns.

Smoothing: A mathematical approach that removes excess data variability while maintaining a (presumably) correct appraisal of the underlying trend.

Spike: A sharp rise in price in a single day or two.

Stochastic: Literally means random. Adopted by some technicians to name process of analyzing closing prices relative to trend direction.

Stock split: A procedure used by management to establish a different market price for its shares by changing the common stock structure of the company. Usually a lower price is desired and established by canceling the outstanding shares and reissuing a larger number of new certificates to current shareholders. The most common ratios are 2-to-1, 3-to-1, and 3-to-2. Occasionally, a higher price is desired and a reverse split takes place when one new share is issued for some multiple number of old shares.

Stop: A contingency order that is placed above the current market price if it is to buy, or below the current market price if it is to sell. A stop order becomes a market order only when the stock or commodity moves up to the price of the buy stop, or down to the price of a sell stop. A stop can be used to enter a new position or exit an old position. *See* Protective stop or Progressive stop.

Stop loss: *See* Protective Stop.

Stop systems: Magee constructed several stop systems — all of them interesting and valuable. These may be classified as follows: (1) support and resistance, (2) trendline, (3) hair-trigger or near progressive stops, and (4) 3-days-away procedure. These are simple for the long-term investor, complex for the speculator. Refer to *Technical Analysis of Stock Trends* (8th ed.).

Supply: Amount of stock available at a given price.

Supply line: *See* Resistance.

Support level: The price level at which a sufficient amount of demand is forthcoming to stop, and possibly turn higher for a time, a downtrend.

Symmetrical triangle: Also called a coil. Can be a reversal or continuation pattern. A sideways congestion where each minor top fails to attain the height of the previous rally and each minor bottom stopping above the level of the previous low. The result is upper and lower boundary lines that converge, if extended, to a point on the right. The upper boundary line must slant down and the lower boundary line must slant up, or it would be a variety of wedge. Volume tends to diminish during formation. Minimum formula: add the widest distance within the triangle to its breakout point.

Tangent: *See* Trendline.

Tape reader: One who makes trading decisions by watching the flow of New York Stock Exchange and American Stock Exchange price and volume data coming across the electronic ticker tape. Today, a day trader.

Tekniplat paper: A specially formatted two-cycle semi-logarithmic graph paper, with sixth-line vertical accents, used to chart stock or commodity prices. (Tekniplat Paper is available at www.johnmageeta.com.)

Test: A term used to describe the activity of a stock or commodity when it returns to, "tests" the validity of a previous trendline or support or resistance level.

Thin issue: A stock that has a low number of floating shares and is lightly traded.

3-day-away rule: A time period used by Edwards and Magee in marking suspected minor tops or bottoms.

Throwback: Return of prices to the boundary line of the pattern after a breakout to the upside. Return after a downside breakout is called a pullback.

Top: *See* Broadening top, Descending triangle, Double top, Head-and-shoulders top, Triple top, and Rounding top.

Trend: The direction prices are moving. *See* Ascending, Descending, and Horizontal parallel trend channels, Convergent trend, Divergent trend, Intermediate trend, Major trend, and Minor trend.

Trend channel: A parallel probable price range centered about the most likely price line.

Trending market: Price moves in a single direction, usually closing at an extreme for the day.

Trendline: A straight line that connects a series of higher lows (an up trendline), a series of lower highs (a downtrend line), or a series of highs and or lows on a horizontal line.

Triangle: *See* Ascending triangle, Descending triangle, Right-angle broadening triangle, and Symmetrical triangle.

Triple bottom: Similar to a flat head-and-shoulders bottom, or rectangle, the three bottoms in a triple bottom.

Triple top: An area pattern with three tops that are widely spaced and with quite deep, and usually rounding, reactions between them. Less volume occurs on the second peak than the first peak, and still less on the third peak. Sometimes called a "W" pattern, particularly if the second peak is below the first and third. The triple top is confirmed when the decline from the third top penetrates the bottom of the lowest valley between the three peaks.

200-day moving-average line: Determined by summing the closing price over the past 200 trading days and dividing by 200, etc.

U/d volume: Is the ratio between the daily up volume to the daily down volume. It is a 50-day ratio determined by dividing the total volume on those days when the stock closed up from the prior day by the total volume on days when the stock closed down.

Uptick: A securities transaction made at a price higher than the preceding transaction.

Uptrend: *See* Ascending trendline and Trend.

Utility average: *See* Dow-Jones Utility Average.

Validity of trendline penetration: The application of the following three tests, when a trendline is broken, to determine whether the break is valid or whether the trendline is still basically intact: (1) the extent of the penetration, (2) the volume of trading on the penetration, and (3) the trading action after the penetration.

Valley: The V-shaped price action that occurs between two peaks. *See* Double top and Triple top.

Volatility: A measure of a stock's tendency to move up and down in price, based on its daily price history over the latest 12-month (or other) period.

Volume: The number of shares in stocks or contracts in commodities that are traded over a specified period.

"W" formation: *See* Triple top.

Wedge: A chart formation in which the price fluctuations are confined within converging straight (or practically straight) lines, but differing from a triangle in that both boundary lines either slope up or slope down. *See* Falling wedge and Rising wedge.

GLOSSARY OF PATTERNS

This section contains chart patterns for the following:

- Major bullish (bottoming patterns)
- Major bearish (topping patterns)
- Major continuation patterns (of previous trend)
- Measurement patterns

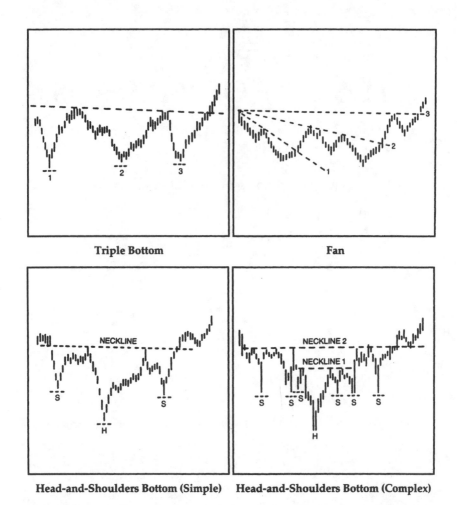

Triple Bottom

Fan

Head-and-Shoulders Bottom (Simple)   **Head-and-Shoulders Bottom (Complex)**

Diagram 21.   Major Bullish (Bottoming) Patterns: Triple Bottom, Fan, Head-and-Shoulders (Kilroy) Bottom (Simple), Head-and-Shoulders (Kilroy) Bottom (Complex). Note usefulness of describing complex H-and-S Bottom a Kilroy Bottom, as various "shoulders" can be described as "fingers."

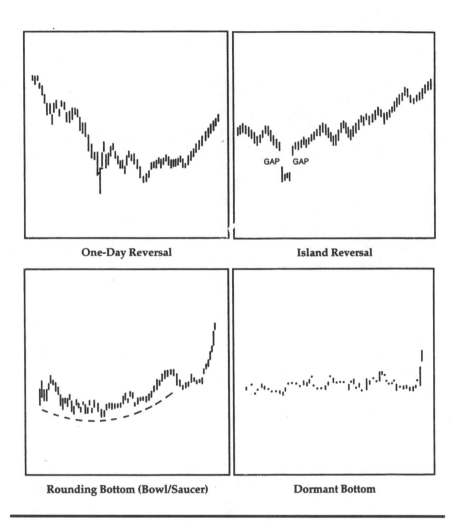

One-Day Reversal

Island Reversal

Rounding Bottom (Bowl/Saucer)

Dormant Bottom

Diagram 22.   Major Bullish (Bottoming) Patterns: 1-Day Reversal, Island Reversal, Rounding Bottom (Bowl/Saucer), and Dormant Bottom.

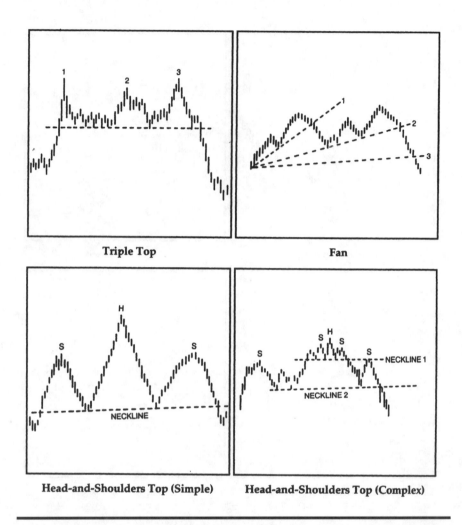

Diagram 23.   Major Bearish (Topping) Patterns: Triple Top, Fan, Head-and-Shoulders Top (Simple), and Head-and-Shoulders Top (Complex).

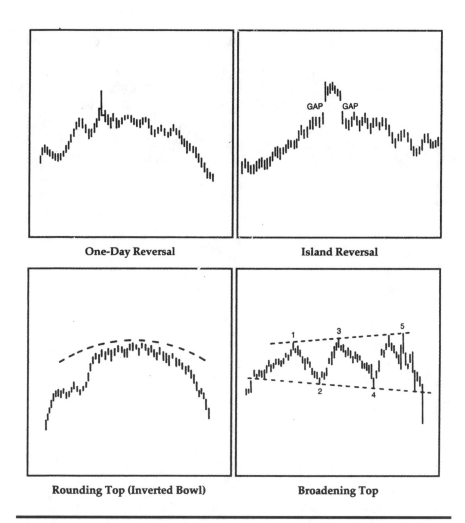

One-Day Reversal

Island Reversal

Rounding Top (Inverted Bowl)

Broadening Top

Diagram 24. Major Bearish (Topping) Patterns: 1-Day Reversal, Island Reversal, Rounding Top (Inverted Bowl), Broadening Top.

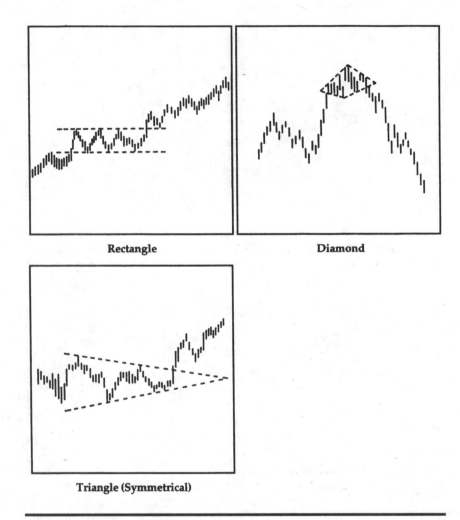

Diagram 25. Indeterminate Patterns: Rectangle, Diamond, and Triangle (Symmetrical).

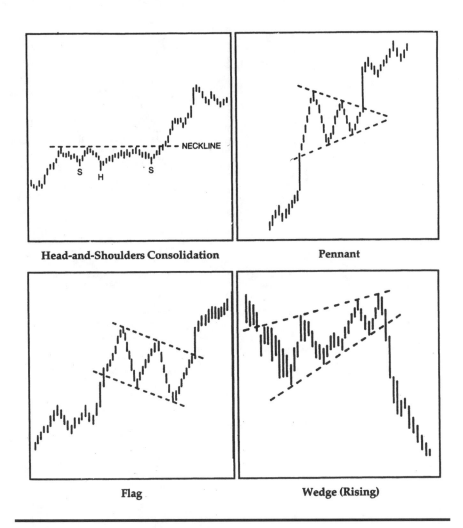

Head-and-Shoulders Consolidation

Pennant

Flag

Wedge (Rising)

Diagram 26. Major Continuation Patterns (of Previous Trend): Head-and-Shoulders (Kilroy) Consolidation, Pennant, Flag, and Wedge (Rising).

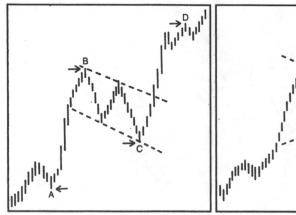

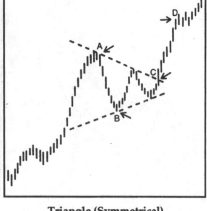

| **Flag** | **Triangle (Symmetrical)** |

Pennants and Flags—The measuring characteristic of these Continuation patterns is a move from the last test of the lower boundary (long) or upper boundary (short) equal to the pole-rally. Graphically, the rally from A to B is repeated from C to D. Generally, these patterns "fly at half mast" and the leg-in will equal the leg-out.

Triangles—When a stock breaks out of a Symmetrical Triangle (either up or down), the ensuing move should carry at least as far as the height of the Triangle as measured along its first Reaction. In the illustration, the measurement is taken from A to B, and the objective plotted by C to D. Right Triangles are measured in similar fashion.

Diagram 27.   Measurement Patterns: Flag and Triangle.

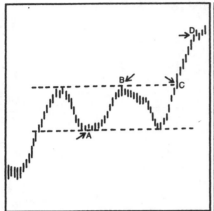 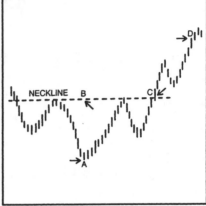

Rectangle

Head-and-Shoulders Bottom

Rectangles—The minimum expectation of breakout C to D (up or down) is equal to the height A to B of the formation.

Head-and-Shoulders Tops/Bottoms—The Head-and-Shoulders formation is one of the most reliable measuring patterns. On either a Top or Bottom the interim target, once the Neckline is penetrated, is the distance from the Top (or Bottom) of the Head to the level of the Neckline directly below (above) the Head. In the illustration, A to B is the measurement and C to D the objective.

Diagram 28. Measurement Patterns: Rectangle, Head-and-Shoulders (Kilroy) Bottom, and Wedge (Rising).

LIST OF DIAGRAMS

LIST OF CHART PATTERNS

INDEX